A. Rowland-Jones

Introduction to the Recorder
A tutor for adults

1478
1978

Oxford University Press
London · Oxford · New York
1978

Preface

This book is intended as a tutor for adult beginners on the descant, treble, or tenor recorder, including those with no previous experience of reading music. The methodology will, however, be of interest to teachers for use in primary schools with additional practice material. The practice pieces in this book are chosen not only for their relevance to technique but to introduce the reader to the delights of the recorder's repertoire.

I should like to thank Barbara Pointon of Homerton College for her advice, Basil Clarke for taking the photographs, my secretary (Margaret Strangward) and my wife for typing the manuscript of this tutor and trying it out among Cambridge teachers. The recorders in the photographs are by Dolmetsch (Haslemere) and Ernst Stieber (Tübingen).

A. Rowland-Jones
Cambridgeshire College of Arts and Technology, Cambridge

1   In this photograph the note treble F (=tenor/descant C) is being played, i.e. all fingers on (0 123 4567). Note that the fingers are roughly parallel, and that the elbows are comfortably beside the body, with the right elbow slightly lower than the left (because the right hand is lower down the instrument). The player looks at his music slightly to one side, projecting sound forward unimpeded to his audience.

Contents

* Notes not in brackets – treble recorder
　Notes in brackets – tenor or descant recorder

Advancing Further

2   Note the angle of the instrument to the body. The wrists are well below the recorder, the left wrist slightly lower than the right. The note being played is treble upper B♭ (=tenor/descant F¹) ∅ 123 4-6-. The second and little fingers of the right hand (i.e. fingers 5 and 7) are raised from their holes, but by less than an inch.

Introductory

Why the Recorder?

It seems that most people start to play the recorder by chance of circumstance rather than because of its sound or the music written for it. An acceptable recorder is cheaper than any other serious musical instrument. It is uncomplicated, and having no overlay of keywork is simple to keep in good playing order; and it is eminently portable. It seems easy to play, and up to a point is so. To anyone feeling they want to take part in music rather than just listen, a recorder in a shop window is therefore a challenge – if others can play it, particularly children, why not I?

If there is already a recorder in the house because a son or daughter plays it at school, the possibility of family music-making is an added incentive. For the recorder is essentially a social instrument. While some attractive but difficult solo music exists, making music with the recorder requires the participation of other players, at least a keyboard or guitar (or lute) accompanist. It is a way of finding friends with a common interest.

Some people are, however, drawn to the recorder because they like its calm sound, others because they are interested in baroque, renaissance, or medieval music. Many newcomers to the recorder, particularly those who associate it only with primary school teaching, are surprised at the range of music it encompasses, including great compositions, often with voices, by Purcell, Bach, Handel, and Telemann. Only during the period 1750 to 1930 does it lack repertoire. Moreover much of the earlier music, including Elizabethan consort pieces, is simple to play, and because it is easier to create a reasonably good note on the recorder than on any other wind instrument a player can in a few weeks reach the point of joining a group of other players to play music that is deeply rewarding. Having reached this level of ability an unambitious player can remain there with relatively little practice, for the challenge in much ensemble music lies more in musical understanding than in technical skill. Yet if he so wishes he can extend his mastery of the recorder to play eighteenth-century and modern sonatas and chamber music, where he will find problems as demanding as he would encounter with other woodwind instruments.

Descant (Soprano), Treble (Alto) or Tenor Recorder?

If you are considering buying this book you probably already possess a recorder. If not, and you want to play both consort and later chamber and solo music, start on the treble. The treble has by far the largest repertoire.

If, however, your interest is restricted to consort playing, you may prefer to start on the tenor provided you can stretch your fingers to cover the holes without strain (many tenors have C keys, but that makes it difficult to get C sharp; some have keys for both C and C sharp). The tenor has a creamy, subdued tone-quality which even beginners find easy to achieve. Moreover, if you play tenor you can very easily switch to descant as both instruments are in C, i.e. that is the note played when all the holes are covered. On the treble all holes covered plays F, and this is the case with the little-used sopranino and with the bass, which has problems of its own.

Schools choose descant because it is cheap, holds its own with the piano, plays the top part and therefore the tune, and fits small hands. But it tends to be over-bearing and shriekish, and good quality tone is hard to achieve. The renaissance descant has a fuller, less piercing tone. There is some concerto material for the baroque descant and strings, but the solo and chamber repertoire for both descant and tenor is very limited. The descant's importance is on the top line of most consort music.

This book attempts to teach the fundamentals of both treble and tenor/descant. In the text the tenor/descant (T/D) references are in brackets, and in Exercises to the right of or after the treble Exercises.

How this book works

This book is intended for self-tuition, but try if you can to get lessons from a qualified teacher. The book does not include the mass of exercises, tunes, or other practice material that one expects in a tutor intended for school use. Instead, on the assumption that you will in any case want to buy and play your own music, it lists pieces in easily available editions to use for practice with another recorder player, or an accompanist. Too much practising on one's own in the early stages often leads to faults in intonation or rhythm that are difficult to eradicate, and does not develop the art of listening to and co-operating with other players in the social process of making music.

Practice exercises are nevertheless given as each new note or group of notes is reached. The extent to which they should be supplemented by other material will depend on your previous musical experience. Unless you already play another wood-wind instrument, you should, however keen you are to get on, pause at the end of Stage 1 (covering most lower-octave notes) to consolidate what you have then learnt by following the suggestions for practice at that point. This will mean buying some music for the purpose according to your interests and who else you can practise with: only the stipulated pieces in those publications should be tackled, but the remaining pieces then become practice material for the end of Stage 2 when you know all the notes. The final section of the book covers some points not dealt with in the two main stages, and suggests various ways of getting on further. Stage 2 should take you to the point of joining the local branch of the Society of Recorder Players, the American Recorder Society, or some other consort group where you will gain experience of recorder playing and develop your musicianship generally.

I can't read a note of music

This can be remedied. As the recorder produces (usually) only one note at a time and all recorders except bass play from the treble clef, you will soon pick up the rudiments needed to play simple recorder music. The Exercises in this book are graded to ease the process, and other practice material is suggested. 'Rudiments' notes on the Exercises are included to help the absolute beginner in music; read all, under both treble and tenor/descant Exercises. They can be ignored by those who learnt to read music at school or who have played another instrument.

In general I have used the whole-note/half-note system of names rather than the semibreve/minim system. It seems simpler and more rational. Those familiar only with the latter will find the two terminologies collated in the list on p.7.

If you feel you need a tutor that incorporates a great deal of gently graded and pleasant solo practice material, though it is without slurs or phrasing, I recommend Hugo Orr's *Basic Recorder Technique* (published by BMI, Canada, and obtainable from Universal Edition in two volumes, both in separate descant (soprano) and treble (alto) versions. It contains some excellent photographs of finger and thumb positions. Walter Bergmann's *Descant Recorder Lessons* (Faber) is less expensive, advances more rapidly than Orr, with the advantage of keyboard accompaniments (in a separate book), but has considerably less explanatory text.

Other books

I recommend Margaret and Robert Donington's *Scales, Arpeggios and Exercises for the Recorder* published by Oxford University Press (OUP). If you intend to get beyond the simple consort music stage, you will need to practise scales, and this should be done with music in front of you. The book is divided into tenor/descant and treble sections, and each exercise is followed by technical notes. Teachers will find useful material in the Teacher's Books of Margo Fagan's *Play Time* primary recorder course (Longman).

Considerable reference is made in the last part of this book to my *Recorder Technique* (shortened to *RT*), also published by OUP, which is of most value to intermediate players wishing to extend their technique; it can therefore be used to follow on from this book. It also contains chapters on the history of the recorder and on the recorder's repertoire.

Before starting to play

If you have a new wooden recorder, it must be 'played in' or it may crack. This means playing for no more than fifteen minutes a day for the first week, then no more than half an hour a day for a week, gradually extending thereafter. After each playing take the instrument apart and dry the bore carefully. Gradually the wood will accommodate to being made moist. Never leave a recorder near a fire or radiator or in the hot sun. But always warm up a recorder (in the hands or pocket), especially the head section, before playing. Blowing into it to warm up defeats the object of dry warmth.

Assemble and take apart a recorder by a gentle clockwise motion. Cork joints should be occasionally greased with lanolin (see also *RT* p.35).

Keep the recorder in a box. Never put it on a chair or table where it can roll off.

Never touch with your finger or anything hard the fipple area of the recorder, i.e. the chamfered 'window' in the head section, the edge and the windway opening opposite the edge. If dirt collects there, clean it away with a soft feather.

Don't hold the recorder by the foot section, as this strains the lower joint.

Fingering

Fingering charts are normally included with new instruments. Tables of normal fingerings are given, for easy reference, on the inside back cover of this book.

Text references to fingerings are on the following system (as in *RT*):

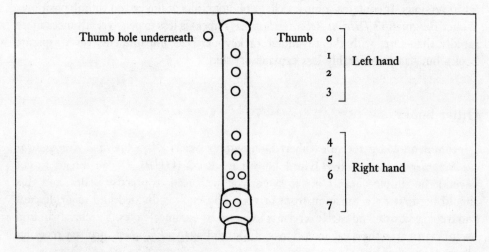

A closed hole is given its number.

An open hole is given a dash.

A partly open hole (or one hole of a double hole) is given its number with a diagonal line through it.

Examples:

0123 4567 = all holes covered.

ø 12−45̸6− = the thumb-hole partly open, the first and second fingers of the left hand covering their holes, but the third not, and the first and second fingers of the right hand covering their holes, with the third finger covering a half-hole and the little finger not covering anything.

Note that the little finger of the left hand is unused, and the thumb of the right hand is used only to support the instrument.

In Stage 1, considerable attention is given to the placing and movement of the fingers and thumbs. This is to mould the hands and fingers into a position where they are most likely to cover the holes and move fluently in rapid passages that will be encountered in later playing. Some people, however, pick up a recorder the very first time in the 'correct' position (and conversely several recorder virtuosi break all the 'rules' to the point of contortionism). These fortunates need not conform to the detailed instructions in Stage 1, the object of which is to cultivate the most relaxed and effective position for the average player.

Stage 1

Holding the recorder

Keeping thumb and fingers away from the window on the head section, join the middle section into the head section with a gentle clockwise motion (one complete revolution is usually adequate). If stiff, grease the joint very slightly. Wash any grease from your fingers. Align the six holes with the window. Similarly join the foot section, leaving the pair of half-holes offset to the right (some descants do not have separate foot sections).

Sitting comfortably straight in a chair without arms, pick up the recorder with the right hand round the middle section so that the right thumb is under the instrument beneath a point halfway between the 4th and 5th holes. If a thumb-rest is fitted, the right thumb should rest underneath it. Now mouth 'oo' so that the lips are rounded with the teeth apart and the tongue well back. Guide the recorder mouthpiece with the left hand to between your lips, much as you would to suck a straw. The instrument should be about halfway between vertical and horizontal. The recorder mouthpiece should never touch the teeth. Give a little experimental blow.

Now let the weight of the instrument settle upon the right thumb and the lower lip. Take the left hand away, and if your recorder already has a thumb-rest you can relax the fingers of the right hand, and raise them slightly. Recorders should have thumb-rests fitted as soon as you have found the best and most comfortable playing position for the right hand. The fingers and the left thumb are then used only for covering holes and not for supporting the instrument. If a thumb-rest is not yet fitted, you will need temporarily to hold the recorder between the thumb and first finger of the right hand, making sure the finger is well away from any hole.

Next, with the instrument firmly supported, put the left thumb not quite vertically under the recorder so that the tip of the thumb-nail touches the joint between the head section and the middle section of the recorder: the flat of the thumb-nail should be facing back towards your chin. The point on the tip of the nail touching the recorder should be a little to the left of centre of the arc of the thumb-nail. Thumbs vary, but getting the thumb position right from the start is crucial to recorder technique.

The left fingers should be poised floating about an inch above the top of the instrument. Slowly and delicately move the whole left hand so that the thumb-nail runs down the barrel of the recorder until it feels the thumb-hole and slips gently into it. Shutting the eyes may help you to concentrate on the sensitivity of the thumb-nail. All fingering should be by feel.

To do this you will have slightly bent the joint of the thumb. Now, very slowly, straighten that joint without changing the position of the hand. What should happen is that the thumb-nail lightly moves over the edge of the thumb-hole, and the flesh of the thumb covers the thumb-hole entirely (see photograph 8 on p.32). The thumb-nail is left almost, but not quite, touching the body of the instrument, so near in fact that a slight upthrust push of the thumb will make such contact. You may have to cut your thumb-nail to achieve these effects, but not too closely.

Set the thumb into its correct position covering the thumb-hole and mentally transfer the point of greatest sensitivity to the soft flesh of the pad of the first finger, not the actual tip of the finger. Looking down the instrument, lower the first finger until it touches the recorder (a traverse of one inch), making sure that the main joint of the finger does not stick up above a horizontal from the finger-nail. Keeping the recorder steady between the right hand and the lips, and the thumb-hole very firmly covered, take the first finger on a voyage of discovery around the edge of the first hole. When it is quite sure exactly where the hole is, centre it and squeeze hard as if trying to prevent something getting out (in a moment that something will be your breath). Now you should be gripping hard between finger and thumb – so hard you can take your right hand away for a moment. Return the right hand for support, and relax the first finger, still covering the hole. Without moving the finger, be aware of the round edge of the hole impinging upon the finger-pad. Alternately press down hard and relax the finger, never uncovering the hole.

Now firmly supporting the recorder between the right thumb and lip, return the first finger of the left hand to the 'poised' point, an inch immediately above the hole. Then with all your concentration (as if swatting a fly) crash down as hard as you can dead on to the hole. A hit on target will be rewarded by a resonant woody

3 Looking down the recorder with all fingers on. Note particularly the position of the first finger with the nail facing straight up, and the angle of the left thumb to the barrel of the recorder (see also photograph 8 on p.32).

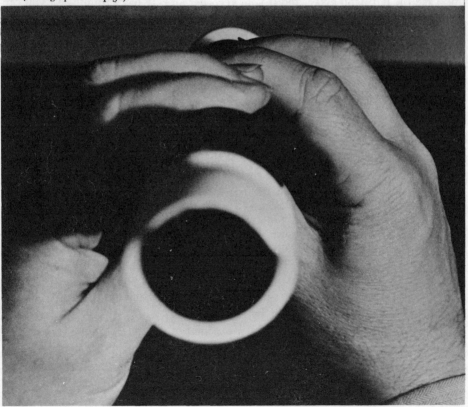

note, like a muffled xylophone. If you miss, try again. In fact try several of these hammer blows until you are sure of hitting the target every time – but don't be tempted to aim from more than an inch away. Keep the other fingers flabbily relaxed and immobile and of course there should be no hand movement. All the work should come from the muscle at the base of the first finger, with no movement from the joints in the finger itself. You can practise this movement at any time you have nothing better to do, each finger independently. Use this 'discover, squeeze, relax, hammer' technique to learn each new fingering. The ultimate objective in covering a hole is for the finger to be relaxed yet the coverage airtight, and in moving a finger for the movement to be short but very rapid and sprightly.

The Note E (T/D B)

Grip the recorder in the thumb and first-finger position now learnt (the thumb-nail just touching the barrel of the recorder because you are squeezing so firmly), and, with lips in the 'oo' position, whisper firmly but gently the word 'do' into the re-corder, using a soft 'd' (as in French or Italian) thus – 'dhoo'. This will produce the note E (B on tenor/descant).

Rudiments
The five lines are called 'the stave'. The positions on them (signifying pitch) are lettered A to G and are as follows:

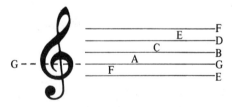

The sign is the treble 'clef' encircling the line G. The note is a quarter note or crotchet – its tail goes either way up.
  The notes of music (signifying length but not pitch) are as follows:

o	Whole note (semibreve)	♪	Eighth note (quaver)
𝅗𝅥	Half note (minim)	♬	Sixteenth note (semiquaver)
♩	Quarter note (crotchet)		Thirty-second note (demisemiquaver)

The names are self-explanatory: there are two eighth notes in a quarter, four in a half note, and so on.

The Note D (T/D A)

Finger E (T/D B), then follow the 'discover, squeeze, relax, hammer' technique until the second hole down is securely covered with the second finger of the left hand on each finger movement. The hammering will produce a 'muffled xylophone' D (T/D A). In covering this hole there are two important things to get right. The first is that the line of the second finger of the left hand should be roughly at right-angles to the line of the recorder (except for a tenor with an offset third hole). Get a friend to check this; and make a deliberate effort to turn the left hand sideways on to the instrument in order to achieve this right-angle (see photograph 2). Secondly, in order to keep the back of the finger from the nail to the main joint fairly flat rather than strongly arched, you must put this second finger slightly further across the instrument than the first, so that the point of coverage is further down the pad of the finger away from the tip. The main joint of the second finger should be level with or only very slightly above horizontal to its nail (see photograph 3 on p.6). You may have to make a slight adjustment in the first-finger position to get the second finger accurately placed.

Remember that the muscular control activating the movement of the second finger comes only from the base of the finger. Concentrate in your mind on isolating that muscle from the muscle at the base of the first finger, as a completely separate part of the digital machine. Remember that the movement is no more than one inch. Try repeated rapid hammerings, watching the finger traverse.

Now, feeling that the thumb-hole and the first and second holes are securely covered, give breath to the note gently but firmly – 'dhoo', holding it long and steady, several times. This is:

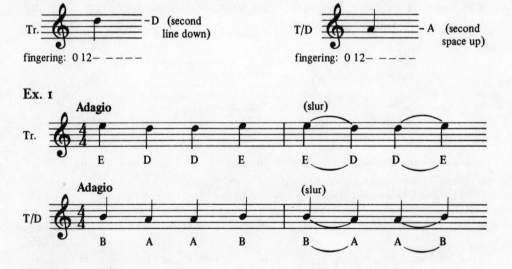

General points

1. Hold the thumb and first finger firmly upon their holes: concentrate upon the muscular movement of the second finger.

2. Think of the hymn 'Christian, canst thou see them', to get the phrasing right. Play notes long and smooth – 'legato'.

3. Note that the finger movement has to be as rapid in the slurs as in the separated notes.

Rudiments

Adagio=rather slow (Presto or Vivace=fast; Allegro=rather fast; Andante=moderate walking speed; Adagio=rather slow; Grave, Largo or Lento=slow).

$\frac{4}{4}$ is the time signature. This is the commonest measure (and therefore often written as 'C') and means four regular beats in each bar, each being of the value of one 'quarter note' ($\frac{1}{4}$ of a whole note). Thus $\frac{4}{4}$ =four quarter notes, the upper figure showing the number of beats, the lower their value. Each bar (shown by the vertical line down the stave) is a repetition of this measure.

Note the extent to which each quarter note, having started regularly on its beat, then takes up its quarter of the bar to accord with the words 'Christ-ian canst thou', the first syllable of 'Christ-ian' being longer than the second. Measure is here established by small variations in the length of each quarter note, as well as by slight differences in the attack upon each quarter note (tonguing) and in their relative loudness. If all four quarter notes were equally emphasized there would be no rhythm, for rhythm consists of an established and repeated measure. In a standard $\frac{4}{4}$ bar greatest emphasis is upon the first beat. There is a secondary emphasis on the third beat; and of the two weak beats the second beat carries a little more weight than the fourth.

If the phrasing (the words 'see' or 'them') requires that one note should run on to another, both notes are taken within one even breath 'dhooo . .' This is called a 'slur'.

The distance ('interval') between the E and D (T/D B and A) used in this piece is called a 'tone'.

The Note C (T/D G)

Still holding the recorder between the lower lip and the right thumb (and finger), and with 0 1 and 2 securely in place, 'discover, squeeze, relax, hammer' with the third finger of the left hand (3) on its hole, hammering a muted C (T/D G). All your thought should now be on the muscle at the base of the third finger (the one that so worried Schumann in his piano playing). The little finger of the left hand can waggle at will – just hold it up out of the way and forget it.

3 should be across the recorder, but not quite as much as 2. The main joint is straighter than 2, so that in looking down the instrument 2 hides 3. Be certain that 2 remains roughly at right-angles. 2 is the positioning finger, and both 1 and 3 should lie comfortably in relation to it.

With the left-hand fingers and thumb carefully in position, squeeze the recorder hard, and then check the marks on your finger-pads made by the rims of the holes. With the fingers straightened they should look something like this:

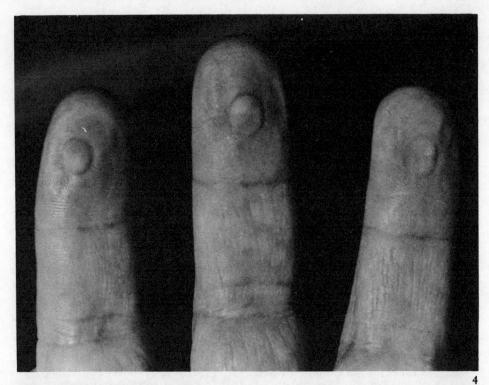

The thumb-hole mark should be:

4
5

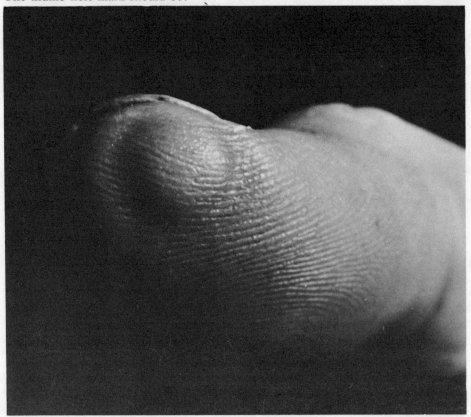

Gently give breath, long and steady, 'dhoo', for

General points

1. Play Ex. 2 in slow march time, with shorter, more separated notes than Ex. 1 (i.e. not legato); but do not play it staccato (short, sharp notes). Differentiate the length and emphasis of the four quarter notes in the bar to establish a firm march rhythm.

2. Take a breath near the end of the fourth bar (marked ✓). Do this in the time remaining between the end of playing the minim and the bar-line. Do not slow down; start the fifth bar in exact co-ordination with the regular walking-pace beat which you have established. There is a phrasing mark (') at the end of the second and sixth bars, but if you start with a big enough breath you should not need to breathe there as well as at the end of the fourth bar. Do not shorten the whole note at the end, or the piece will sound unbalanced.

3. If a note does not strike, it is because you are blowing too hard or not covering the holes properly. 1 may have slipped in your efforts to cover 3, for example. If you encounter this trouble, go back to your 'discover, press, relax, hammer' exercise until the fingers become familiar with their exact positions for your instrument.

Rudiments

C and D (D/T G and A) are, like D and E (D/T A and B), one tone apart.
C – D – E (D/T G – A – B) plays 'doh, ray, me' of the tonic sol-fa scale.

Ex. 3 *Here's a health unto his Majesty*

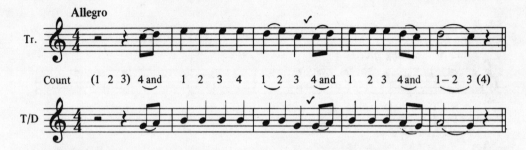

General points

1. Remember that your fingers must move even more nimbly when playing slurs than for the separated notes.
2. Take the breath in bar 3, even if you can manage without it. You will have to take in air through the mouth very quickly in order not to be late for the eighth notes or shorten the preceding quarter note unduly.

Rudiments

This tune starts on the fourth beat of a bar. The first three beats are silent. Silence in music is shown by 'rests' which with their equivalent value notes are as follows:

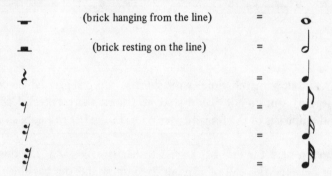

Differentiate the emphasis upon each of the four quarter notes in the second bar – 'health un-tó his'. Note the joined-up eighth notes ♫ = ♪ ♪ . Sixteenth notes and thirty-second notes join similarly ♬ ♬ . Interpose a quick 'and' between your beats to get the feel of the eighth notes.

Ex. 4 *Minuet*

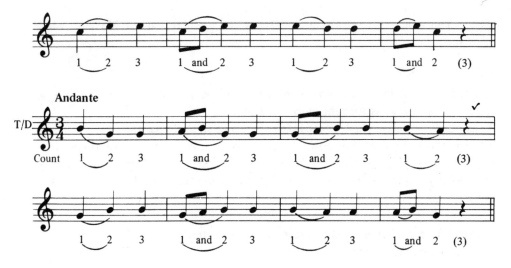

General points

1. In bar 1 imagine you have an elastic band round fingers 2 and 3 so that they drop on their holes together. If they do not, you will hear an intrusive 'in-between note'. This must be eradicated.
2. In bar 2 put the imaginary elastic band on 2 and 3 the moment you have lifted 2.
3. Bar 5 contains an upward two-finger slur. Press 1 down firmly and relax 2 and 3. Pretend they are one finger and then throw them upwards from their holes.
4. Three beats (quarter notes) to the bar. In a minuet rhythm the three beats have descending emphasis by length (and/or by attack and loudness). The last quarter note in each bar in Ex. 4 is therefore short. But in a waltz (Ex. 6) the third beat is stronger than the second.
5. Note the rests in bars 4 and 8. Do not play the preceding quarter note as a half note.
6. The breath-mark falls on a rest. Use the opportunity to full advantage.

Ex. 5 Edmund Rubbra *Air*

Treble only

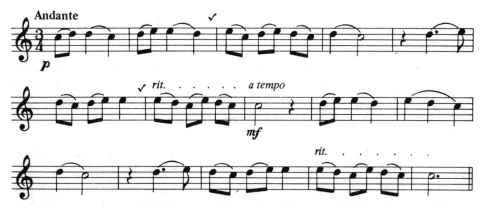

This is No. 1 of Rubbra's *First Study Pieces* for treble recorder and piano (Lengnick). The rests at the beginning of bars 5 and 12 should be very palpable moments of silence. You should take breaths at the rests as well as where marked. Make the whole piece sing.

Rudiments
A dot after a note increases its value by a half. Thus $\dot{}$ and $\dot{}$
Note that ♩. ♪♩ is thought of as '1 2 and 3'.
A dot above or below a note means play short and sharp (staccato).
'rit.' (ritardando) means slow down. 'a tempo' means resume the previous speed.
p (piano)=soft *f* (forte)=loud *mp* (mezzo piano)=fairly soft *mf* (mezzo forte)= fairly loud *pp* (pianissimo)=very soft *ff* (fortissimo)=very loud (not in recorder music).

cresc(endo)=grow louder   *decr*(escendo)=grow softer.
Volume changes are referred to as 'dynamics'.

Ex. 6 Tenor/Descant only Robert Salkeld *First Waltz*

This piece is taken from Robert Salkeld's *First Concert Pieces* for descant, treble, and piano (Schott). Practise it up to a fast Viennese waltz speed. Then try it with each of the first six bars slurred (avoid an intrusive A in bar 4).

Breathing

Recorder playing is compounded of four elements; fingering (and thumbing), breath control, tonguing, and . . . musicianship. Up to now this book has concentrated only on the first.

You may have had difficulty in keeping your long notes steady. Try to imagine your breath proceeding into the recorder windway as a steadily moving column of air generated from the base of your lungs (the diaphragm) and passing at the same gentle flow through your throat and mouth, a different action from blowing (or puffing) from the throat.

You need about as much breath for recorder playing as you would for making a speech or reading poetry aloud. Draw in breath quickly but deeply through the mouth at a breath mark, rest, or end of phrase: do not gasp or swallow air. Do not, however, take in so much air that its exhalation is hard to control. The rate at which you exhale into the recorder can be judged by breathing out through rounded lips on to the back of your hand about three inches away from your mouth. The effect should be to warm the hand; if it cools it, then you are probably blowing too hard.

But exactly how hard you blow depends on your instrument, narrow-windway recorders requiring higher breath-pressures. The right breath-pressure is that which produces the best-sounding note. The low notes require a little less breath-pressure than the high ones.

Play each of the notes you know with slightly varying breath-pressures until you produce the most beautiful round note, neither too edgy nor too whispy. Listen very carefully to get this right – play into the corner of a room so that all your sound is reflected back to you. For each note this indicates the normal breath-pressure. Learn it by playing beautiful steady notes as part of your practice.

For the time being, until you master advanced techniques to compensate for intonation (=tuning) changes, a *very* slightly higher breath-pressure than the normal for each note must do for *f* (forte), and *very* slightly lower for *p* (piano). Do not go sharp or flat. But *imagine* volume differences (as in the Rubbra piece) to give life and plasticity to your playing.

Important note for beginners in reading music
You are now ready to play three-note pieces. If you could not previously read music, practise the following music **with another player**, before advancing further with this book. Some of these pieces are inevitably for school use but are nevertheless enjoyable to play. If you have had no difficulty in reading the music so far, go straight on to the Note A (T/D E) below.

Tenor/Descant and Piano:
  Walter Bergmann *Descant Recorder Lessons* (Faber) Nos. 1-21
Descant and Treble:
  Walter Bergmann *Initial Duets*, Book I (Faber) Nos. 1-3
Descant, Treble and Piano:
  Robert Salkeld *First Concert Pieces* (Schott Ed. 10172) Nos. 1-4 and first 11 bars of No. 6 (Ex. 6 above)
Treble and Piano:
  Edmund Rubbra *First Study Pieces* (Lengnick) No. 1 Air (Ex. 5 above)
  Colin Hand *Come and Play* (OUP) No. 1 Spring Song
Descant and Piano, with Descant 2 (8 notes) and Treble (6 notes) ad lib.:
  J. J. Rousseau 'Air on Three Notes' in Walter Bergmann's *School Ensemble Book* (Schott)
The other pieces in all these books will supply later needs.

The Note A (T/D E)

With the left-hand fingers and thumb firmly in position for C (T/D G), but not squeezed, transfer attention to your right hand. Resting the recorder on the lower lip, firmly place the middle finger of the right hand (5) on the fifth hole down the recorder so that it is at right-angles to the instrument (see photo no. 1). Cover the hole well down the pad of the finger towards the first joint line so that the back of the finger is flat, not arched, and is horizontal (photograph 3 on p.6). Now grip the recorder with the right thumb and middle finger strongly and remove the left hand altogether; then try to take all the weight of the recorder between the right middle finger and thumb so that you can hold the recorder slightly away from your mouth (easily done with the descant but precarious with the tenor). This confirms the position of the right thumb supporting the instrument. With a tenor your middle finger may be more relaxed if it is not quite at right-angles, but very slightly pointing down the recorder. Nevertheless try to get your hand as far round to sideways as you can comfortably manage. The right wrist should be as much, or almost as much, beneath the recorder as the left wrist. Return the left hand to C (T/D G) to check this. The thumbs and forearms should be in line and the elbows should be near, but not touching, the body.

'Discover, press, relax, and hammer' with 5. When you have it truly positioned, hold it down firmly and repeat the process with 4. This can be awkward, especially with the tenor, and you may need to roll the finger slightly so that the nearside of the pad, rather than the centre, covers the hole. Still holding 5 down, hammer with 4 until you feel you are in position. Now, coupling the two fingers together in your imagination, hammer both together. When you create a woody resonant A (T/D E) with each hammer-blow, give long breath to the instrument, playing

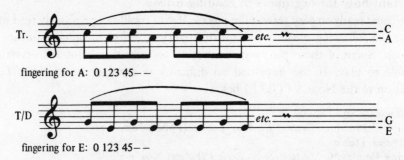

fingering for A: 0 123 45 – –

fingering for E: 0 123 45 – –

Do not let the right hand swing round towards you from its sideways position during this process, otherwise you will later have difficulty in using fingers 6 and 7.

Ex. 7 *Skye Boat Song* (middle section)

General points

1. Play as if you were singing the words, with a full but quiet tone. You will need to breathe deeply to play each four bars in one breath.
2. Bar 2 has a difficult D and A interval (T/D A and E), involving the third finger of the left hand (3) and the first and second of the right (4 and 5). Hold 0 12 down very firmly for the D (A). Relax 3 4 and 5 and let them drop together. For the upward movement let them drop (upwards) off the recorder. Play this bar more and more slowly with well separated notes until you eradicate intrusive notes between D and A (T/D A and E): you may have to play it so slowly that you actually feel the fingers in place before you blow the note. Then become more legato and work back to the right speed of the piece.
3. When you feel confident about the finger movements, try slurring the first half of each bar.
4. You may sometimes find that a low note such as A (E) does not strike. It could be that you are tonguing or blowing too hard. But it is more likely that you are not covering the holes – perhaps a finger of the *left* hand has slipped. Keeping the fingers down, feel round the rim of each hole in turn, starting with 1, and you will locate the leaking finger. Exercise it with the 'discover, press, relax, hammer' method.

Rudiments

This piece has six beats in a bar, and each beat is an eighth note – not a quarter note. The six beats are counted 123456. Played more quickly this develops into two beats (1 and 4) in the bar. Note that ♩. = six beats if the piece is played slowly, two beats if the piece is played quickly. Similarly you will encounter $\frac{12}{8}$ (see Ex. 23) – four slow beats each divided into three, and $\frac{9}{8}$ – three slow beats each divided into three. $\frac{3}{8}$ indicates a faster triple time than $\frac{3}{4}$, and may be counted as only one beat (divided in three) to a bar. The joining up of the eighth notes in threes reminds you of the grouping.

The Note G (T/D D)

Discovering the sixth hole, holding 0 123 45 down, is simplified in that on most instruments it is slightly recessed; but it is complicated in that it is a double hole. If, however, your right hand is well sideways on to the instrument, the coverage of 6 should be so far down the fleshy pad of the finger as to be quite near the bone of the first joint, and 6 therefore goes well across the instrument, straddling the double holes (see photograph 6 on p.18). Accurate hammering with no other finger leaking produces a very rewarding resonant G (D) sound. Give breath gently, for G (D) usually has a powerful, dominating tone-quality.

fingering: 0 123 456–

fingering: 0 123 456–

Now that six holes are covered, check your finger position according to the instructions of *The Second Book of the Flute Master Improv'd*, published about 1730 – 'Observe in the foregoing Instructions for holding the Flute' (i.e. recorder) 'that you keep your fingers on a Direct Line from ye holes they Stop, neither bringing your Nuckles higher or lower but eaven with your fingers ends which will give every finger a greater Comand of ye holes it stops & is much hansomer for Sight'.

6 Bearing in mind the size and shape of your hands and fingers in relation to your instrument, and what is most comfortable for you personally to play effectively, compare by looking in a mirror the position of each of your fingers with that of each finger in this photograph. All holes are covered. Note how the fingers form a 'plateau'.

Ex. 8 'On the Queensland Railway Lines' (penultimate bar slightly changed) from *Australian Bush Tunes* (J. S. Manifold) for descant recorder and guitar (Schott Ed. 10767)

General points

1. Bar 2 involves making all three fingers of the right hand fall off upwards at once. Press the left-hand fingers down firmly on their holes in readiness for fingering C (G) and relax the right-hand fingers just before their leap takes place.
2. Bar 4 has the same A to D (E to A) movement as bar 2 of Ex. 7.

Rudiments

Scherzando means (literally) 'jokingly'. When you have mastered the notes and the finger movements, this piece should swing along joyfully. To get the rhythm right, apply the words of the title to the first two bars, emphasising 'On'. Beat two quarter notes in a bar (duple time). If you give equal stress to the first note of each $\frac{2}{4}$ bar it will not subside into $\frac{4}{4}$. $\frac{4}{4}$ is more firm and broad; $\frac{2}{4}$ is more 'lifted' and short-winded.

The Note F¹ (T/D C¹)

Play C (T/D G) o 123 ----; remove the third finger of the left hand playing D (A), and then the first finger. This gives the note F¹ (C¹). It is a 'cross-fingering' (i.e. a hole or holes are covered below an open hole).

It is easy to slur from D to F¹ (T/D A to C¹) in either direction because only one finger (1) moves:

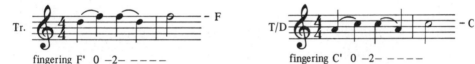

fingering F¹ 0 -2- ----   fingering C¹ 0 -2- ----

But you should practise the movement from E to F¹ (D/T B to C¹) which involves taking off 1 and putting down 2 simultaneously. The slightest fault in co-ordination will create an unwanted in-between note (D or F♯¹) (D/T A or C♯¹). Practise the movement without blowing, first keeping 3 down, then without 3. Then play the following, first with the notes well separated, then slurred (as in brackets):

Feel you are making a little skip as your fingers move – tripping neatly from one note to the other.

Finally practise in the same way the movement C to F¹ (T/D G to C¹). Hold the F¹ (C¹) firmly and 1 and 3 very lightly immediately before making the move, and then activate 1 and 3 to fall on to or off the recorder:

Do not be disheartened if the slur does not come neatly every time: even experienced players have trouble with such slurs as C to F¹ (T/D G to C¹) or D to A (T/D A to E) – see Ex. 7 note 2.

Ex. 9 Hymn tune 'Sussex' (penultimate bar slightly changed) *English Hymnal* No. 385

General points

1. Even in a slow hymn tune the fingers must move nimbly, especially in slurs. Sluggish finger movement in fact sounds even worse in slow music than fast.
2. Phrase according to the words – try and get something of the meaning of the words into your playing (e.g. play the last line 'rejoicingly'). But do not let your dynamics push you out of tune.
3. Take a good breath at the end of each line, as if you were singing the hymn. Give the whole notes their full value.
4. Aim at a rich tone-quality.
5. The tenor/descant version is that in the *English Hymnal*. Play it with keyboard if possible.

Rudiments

The beat is four half notes to the bar. A half-note beat usually represents a more ponderous gait than a quarter-note beat, but not necessarily slower.

Listen carefully to the intervals between C and D (E and A), and D and E (A and B) which are both tones, and that between E and F¹ (B and C¹) which is a semitone. A major scale consists of two groups of four notes, each separated as follows: tone – tone – semitone. Thus, C D E͞ F͞ are the first four notes of the C major scale (T/D G A B͞ C͞ are the first four notes of the G major scale).

Ex. 10 from Handel's *Harp Concerto*

Tr.

Count   1 2 3 and 4 and   1

T/D

Count   1 2 3 and 4 and   1

General point

When you can play this accurately with separated notes, try slurring C D E F⁺
(T/D G A B C⁺).

Rudiments

C = $\frac{4}{4}$

To start a piece off the beat, as here, imagine during the rests that the music has already inexorably started like a train, and jump on as it moves forward. The spring for the jump is taken on the third beat (the eighth-note rest).

The eighth note on beat 4 is more accented than the eighth notes on the two 'ands'. Remember the accentuation for the all-quarter-note bars 2 and 4. Hold the half notes for almost their full value.

In the treble version a ♭ precedes the time signature. This is a flat, which lowers a note it precedes by a semitone. If it is put at the beginning of a line of music after the clef that note is always flattened. This is called the key signature as it tells you the key of the music (i.e. the note or chord the music is likely to finish on).

The treble version of this Handel excerpt is in F major. The interval between A and B is a tone, so in F major, B has to be flat (in compliance with the rudiment note on Ex. 9) to create a semitone interval between the two notes at the end of the first half of the F major scale, thus (semitones bracketed) F G A B♭ C D E F. Now look back to the tenor/descant version of Ex. 9. This is in G major (G is the last note). In G major F has to be sharp to comply with the major scale rule, as the interval between F and G is a tone: G A B C D E F♯ G.

If, because of the melody or harmony, the composer does not wish a sharp or flat in a key signature to apply, he makes the note 'natural' by putting ♮ before it. Or he may wish you to play a note sharp or flat even though it is not made so by the key signature: he then puts ♯ or ♭ before the note. The three 'accidental' signs so used apply to their note for the rest of the bar, but in the next bar the note reverts to what it normally is by the key signature.

If F is sharpened in the key signature by the ♯ on the top line of the stave, it applies to other Fs, e.g. the F in the space between the two bottom lines of the stave. All sharps or flats in the key signature operate similarly.

The treble version of Ex. 9 and the tenor/descant version of Ex. 10 are in C major, which has no sharps or flats: C D E F G A B C.

One note sharpened plays the same sound as the next note up flattened, so G♯

and A♭ sound the same; a piano keyboard illustrates this.

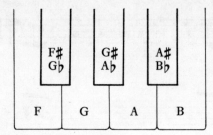

The Note G¹ (T/D D¹)

This is the middle G¹ (D¹) an octave above bottom G (D)=0 123 456–.

With the instrument firm between right thumb and lower lip, play F¹ (C¹). Now, playing a long F¹ (C¹), relax the left thumb, and let it suddenly drop off straight downwards to half an inch below its hole; continue blowing into the instrument. Do not bend the thumb joint – the only muscular movement should be at the base of the thumb. You have now played

Putting the thumb back quickly and accurately is more difficult. Avoid moving the thumb more from the vertical, as this would make you cover the hole with the flat

7 Thumb off position. Compare this with photographs 8 and 9 on pp.32 and 33 to see how little movement there is between the three thumb positions (on, off, thumbed).

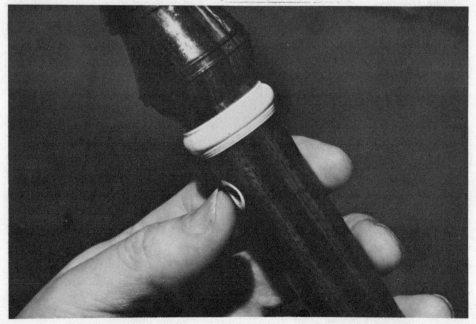

of the thumb-pad; the covering position should always be with the thumb-nail almost touching the instrument (see photographs nos. 8 and 9). Try hammering exercises with the thumb, keeping six fingers down. Play this Exercise (A), first as it is, then with pairs of notes and finally whole bars slurred.

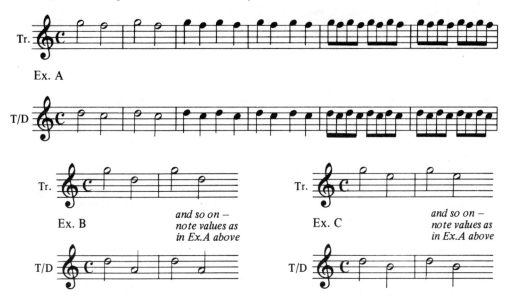

Watch the synchronization of tonguing and thumb movement in the eighth-note section.

Repeat the exercise using D (A) instead of F¹ (C¹), i.e. Ex. B above. Then try using E (B), i.e. Ex. C above – this is difficult. Work through the three exercises again but with the two notes reversed (i.e. starting Ex. A on F¹ (C¹)). Every so often stop suddenly in the middle of an exercise to make sure the thumb has not moved into the 'flat' position. Keep the thumb movement to half an inch or less on and off its hole.

Ex. 11 'Kilt thy coat, Maggie' No. 12 from *Fifty Old Airs and Dances from Scotland and Ireland* for descant recorder solo (Schott)

General point

Where the first note of the bar is shorter than the note on the second beat (e.g. the first bar of Ex. 11 opens with an eighth note, and the second beat is a quarter note), the first beat should be heavily accentuated. In this piece the accentuation permeates the whole piece – the first beat of the first, third, and alternate bars throughout should be stressed. This makes it all the more important to play the E – G¹ (B – D¹) slur neatly; if you have difficulty, repeat the preceding Ex. C in its E – G¹ (B – D¹) slurred version.

Rudiments

The two dots at the end of the first line mean repeat from the beginning (or from the last double bar). D.C. (da capo) means 'from the head' – i.e. go back to the beginning, and play as far as 'Fine' (finish).

Note the key signature in the T/D version (G major); but there are in fact no Fs in the piece to sharpen.

Tonguing

Play each of your four new notes F¹ G¹ A and G (T/D C¹ D¹ E and D) long and slow several times with varying breath-pressure, to establish the ideal tone-quality for each (see p.15). In this process you will discover that the two lower notes sound best when started with a softer tonguing than the two higher notes, although the difference is very tiny. Ensure that your tongue is correctly placed. Before the note starts, the tip of the tongue should be grazing the ridge in the hard palate above the upper teeth, just sufficiently to impede the passage of air. The note is started – 'tongued' – by drawing the tongue back from the teeth-ridge quickly but very gently. The note is stopped by returning the tongue in exactly the same manner to its 'grazing the teeth-ridge' position. Practise this by having the recorder at your lips in the playing position but letting through so meagre a flow of air that it is not sufficient to create a note.

Practice material

You now know seven notes – G¹ F¹ E D C A and G (T/D D¹ C¹ B A G E and D), and before going on to four other notes of the lower octave, completing Stage 1 of this book, you may like to consolidate with practice material. This is not essential for players who started with some musical knowledge and feel they are progressing well.

Tenor/Descant solo:
    C. M. Mullins   *Fifty Old Airs and Dances* (Schott) Nos. 1 and 5 – see Ex. 11
Tenor/Descant and Piano:
    W. Bergmann   *Descant Recorder Lessons* (Faber) Nos. 22-28, 37-39, 41-45
Descant and Treble:
    W. Bergmann   *Initial Duets*, Book I (Faber) Nos. 4-8 (and descant 9-11)
Descant, Treble and Piano:
    R. Salkeld   *First Concert Pieces* (Schott) Nos. 5-7
Treble and Piano:
    E. Rubbra   *First Study Pieces* (Lengnick) Nos. 2 and 3
    C. Hand   *Come and Play* (OUP) Nos. 2-8
Descant/Tenor, Guitar and other instruments:
    J. S. Manifold   *Australian Bush Tunes* (Schott) 'I've just come from Sydney'

The Notes E♭ and B   (T/D B♭ and F♯)

Flattening of notes in the lower octave is effected by leaving a hole open then adding two fingers as a cross-fingering. Thus E (B) is o 1-- ----, and E♭ (B♭) is o 1-3 4---. Most of the flattening required is caused by 3, but not quite enough for a full semitone, so 4 has to be added. Although 4 is not critical, make 3 and 4 drop together by imagining that they are yoked together. Try a hammering exercise and the resultant muffled xylophone noise will show whether the fingers are together or not. Then slur E to E♭ and back (T/D B to B♭). Now try the complex movement of D – E♭ – F¹ (D/T A – B♭ – C¹), as follows:

You may experience difficulty in this movement. Play the piece first slowly and with the notes well detached, and only play legato, and ultimately slurred, later.

    C (T/D G) is also flattened by adding two fingers, thus o 123 -56-. Follow the same process as for E♭ (B♭). As the interval between B and C is a semitone, flattening C by a semitone produces B.

    On tenor/descant, flattening G by a semitone produces G♭ which is not much used in recorder music. But G♭ is the same sound as the important note F♯.

Ex. 12 Coventry Carol (No. 22 in *The Oxford Book of Carols*)

General point
Sing the words to yourself as you play.

Rudiments
This piece has no time signature as it is irregular: the beat is in half notes. Pause slightly at the end of each line of verse (shown by the capital letter for the next line). The number of beats in the bars is 4, 3, 3, 3; 3, 2, 3, 3, 3; 3, 2, 2.

It is in a minor key (treble C minor, tenor/descant G minor). The intervals of the first four notes of a minor scale are: tone, semitone, tone. Thus A minor (which has no sharps or flats) starts A B C D. Play this up and down to feel the difference between it and the major scale G A B C. Music in the minor usually sounds sadder than music in the major. You can generally tell a piece in the minor because of the sharps in the body of the music; the leading note (i.e. the penultimate note of the scale) has to be sharpened. This often tells you the key of the piece, as the key-note ('tonic') is the one above the sharpened leading note. Thus the tenor/descant version of Ex. 12 has an F♯, showing it is in G minor. The treble version is in C minor (the B♭ in the key signature has to be sharpened to B♮ at the leading notes).

Memorize the following key signatures:

Note that the relative minor (i.e. the one with the same key signature) is two notes lower than its major. In the key signatures with three or more accidentals, sharps step up, flats step down.

The Notes F♯¹ and C♯ (T/D C♯¹ and G♯ or A♭)

The lower octave two-finger flattening applies. Thus F♯¹ (C♯¹) is − 12− −−−− (a flattened form of G¹ (D¹)), and C♯ or D♭ (G♯ or A♭) is o 12− 45−−. Practise them within scale passages, slow and well separated at first, then legato, and ultimately slurred:

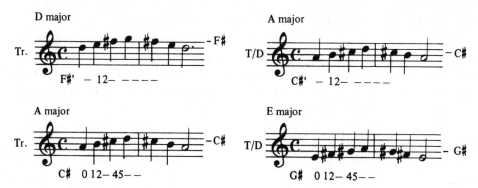

For the movement F♯¹ to E (T/D C♯¹ to B) imagine that the 'thumb on, second finger off' movement is pivoting about the first finger which is stationary.

In the difficult A major (E major) exercise, the second finger of the right hand, which remains down except for D (A), can be the pivot about which the complex cross-finger movements gyrate. Hold the pivot finger down firmly and keep the moving fingers relaxed.

Ex. 13 G. F. Handel *Bourrée* from Flute Sonata in G (penultimate bar slightly changed)

General points

1. Play softly and trippingly, quite slowly in $\frac{4}{4}$ at first, then faster, counting two minims in a bar.
2. All music based on dances should be played as if you were playing it for actual dancers, helping them to lift their feet to the rhythm of the dance and to be no longer earthbound.

Rudiments

The key signature sharpens *all* the F's (T/D all the Fs and C's). In bar 5 all the Cs (Gs) are sharpened as the first sharp applies to the whole bar.

The dots over or under the notes indicate staccato – play short, and with light tonguing. They apply throughout the piece although only given for the first bar. > means stressed. A strong stress is indicated by '*sf*'=sforzando.

Even though written C (=$\frac{4}{4}$) a Bourrée has *two* beats to the bar, so that when played at the proper speed (do not try this until you are really sure of the notes and can finger *all* the eighth notes neatly) it would become two half-note beats to the bar. When you have four eighth notes in duple time, as in the first bar, only the first is accented – there is no secondary accent on the third.

A Bourrée, and its close relation, the Gavotte (which starts in the middle of the bar, not at the end – see Ex. 21), is normally written in duple time – $\frac{2}{2}$ or $\frac{2}{4}$, ¢, or even just 2. The C time-signature here suggests this Bourrée should not be played too fast.

Note that there are only three quarter notes in the last bar; the fourth is made up by the odd quarter note at the beginning of the piece.

Practice material

At this point, even if you have earlier experience in music, you should not proceed further until you have consolidated the eleven notes you now know. Make opportunities to play with other people. What you practise will depend on your interests and whom you can play with, but the following list may be helpful:

Tenor/Descant solo:
  C. Mullins *Fifty Old Airs and Dances*, Vol. 1 (Schott) Nos. 1, 2, 5, 12 (Ex. 11), and 25 (difficult)
Tenor/Descant and Piano:
  W. Bergmann *Descant Recorder Lessons* (Faber) Nos. 22-8, 37-9, 41-5, 56-7, 59 and 60
  Appleby and Fowler Book 1 of *Oxford Books of Recorder Music* (OUP) – all pieces and first two of Book 2
Descant and Treble:
  James Hook *Easy Lessons* (ed. Bergmann) (Schott Ed. 10359) – the first seven of this book of 18th-century pieces
  M. Duschenes (arr.) *Easy Duets* (Universal – BMI Canada) Nos. 1-10
Two Trebles:
  Jean de Castro Nos. 3, 4, and 5 in *Hortus Musicus* 4 (Bärenreiter) – for those with some experience in reading music
Treble and Piano:
  E. Rubbra *First Study Pieces* (Lengnick)
  Freda Dinn *First Study Pieces* (Lengnick) – these are useful elementary technical exercises
  Appleby and Fowler *Oxford Books of Recorder Music*, Book 10 (OUP) – all pieces except No. 8

Stage 2

The music in Stage 2 is chosen not only to illustrate technical points and provide exercise, but also to serve as an introduction to the recorder player's standard repertoire. For the treble it includes both consort music and solo pieces. The tenor/descant exercises are drawn mainly from consort music.

Separate rudiments notes are not given in Stage 2, but a few new points are covered in the notes on the Exercises.

The Notes F and B♭ (T/D C and F)

These two notes bring the little finger of the right hand into use. Refer to p.17 and finger G (D) o 123 456–, remembering to keep 6 well across the instrument. Play G (D) to check that your fingering is firm. Without moving the hand, drop the little finger to cover both the double-holes with the soft pad of the finger; keep the little finger straight (see photograph 6 on p.18). If the drop is accurate and the holes are in the best position for the length of your finger, this should produce a 'muffled xylophone' F (C). If it does, hold the little finger firmly down, feeling the pressure generated from the muscle at the base of the finger, and tonguing very gently and blowing softly, play F (C). If the muffled xylophone note does not sound, grope around with the little finger feeling for the holes, concentrating on the sensitivity of the fleshy pad of the finger. You may need to twist the foot-joint slightly one way or the other. Keep experimenting until you have it in the best position. When you are sure you have it right, mark it with a thin felt marker so that you always align the foot section to this position when assembling the instrument. Every so often in this process check that all the other fingers are covering their holes by playing G (D) – it is all too easy for a left-hand finger to slip while you concentrate on a right-hand fingering.

When you have the position right, consolidate by the customary 'discover, squeeze, relax, hammer' procedure. Do not let the right hand swing round towards you in the process. The hammering exercise is especially important to strengthen the weak muscle of the little finger. It can be practised at any time by holding the first three fingers of the right hand against each other, and moving the little finger up and down independently, keeping it straight.

When the fingering is sure, experiment with different breath-pressures and tonguing to play the richest possible bottom note. The tonguing may have to be very light for the note to strike, but the split second it has begun insinuate a higher breath-pressure to achieve the optimum tone-quality. After the note has spoken, blow increasingly hard so that you discover at what breath-pressure the note breaks (or overblows) to middle C (or thereabouts). It will begin to rasp before it actually overblows. The best tone-quality is usually at a breath-pressure just less than the point where the note begins to rasp. Recorders vary considerably in their behaviour on the bottom note. A good recorder in the hands of a good player can produce a bottom F (C) which is as loud as a softly played F^{II} (C^{II}) two octaves higher.

Bb (F) is played simply by lifting 5 –

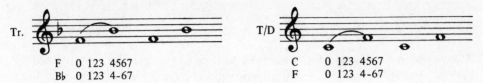

F	0 123 4567
Bb	0 123 4-67

C	0 123 4567
F	0 123 4-67

This note needs the same light tonguing as F (C) but should be creamed up with higher breath-pressure the moment it has struck to achieve optimum tone-quality. Note that Bb (F) follows the normal 'two fingers below' rule of a cross-fingering in the lower octave. It will play, but should not be played, without 7; on most instruments this gives a slightly sharp Bb (F).

Ex. 14 Tr. G. F. Handel *Passepied* No. 3 in *Easy Dances* for treble recorder and piano ed. Hillemann (Schott Ed. 2563A)

Notes

1. A passepied is a fast dance with a strong beat at the beginning of each bar – almost a one in a bar beat. But play this slowly at first to get the Fs and Bbs right – and the difficult finger moves involving Eb (don't forget the key signature!). Do not rush the sixteenth notes in bar 5: play the awkward A to Bb move, involving three fingers of the right hand, slowly with separated notes before attempting the fast slur.

2. Note the repeated sections: and the pattern of phrases formed by breaths taken after the second beat, except for one place to give variety and interest – Handel was a master of such subtleties. The last four bars should be taken in one breath to offset the shortness of the phrase at the end of the first section.

3. The book from which this piece is taken is the recorder player's first step towards playing Handel sonatas. Play it with the keyboard accompaniment; if with piano, ask your accompanist to play softly (especially the right hand) or he may tempt you into blowing too hard for good tone.

Ex. 15 T/D Anthony Holborne *Paradizo* (last strain) (Schott Archive 50) – descant part

Notes

1. This is from Holborne's five-part consort music *Pavans, Galliards, Almains and other short Aeirs for Viols, Violins, or other Musicall Wind Instruments*, published in 1599 ('other'=otherwise). It goes well on recorders and you will certainly play much of this music in a recorder consort group.

2. This piece is a Pavan and should have four stately beats to the bar. Play it very slowly at first to get the Fs and Cs right, especially the F – E moves. Make sure you cover all the right-hand holes in the G – C move at the beginning of bar 4.

3. Count very carefully, especially the rests. Don't be caught out by the rhythmic change in the two similar phrases round bar 3. The commas represent phrasing without the need to take a breath. Note the four-note group across a bar, typical of pavans.

4. Bar 6 contains a 'tie', more often used to join a note which continues across a bar. It could here have been expressed as a quarter note, but then would be more unexpected to read.

5. Hold the last note steadily and quietly for four full beats.

6. Note the small 8 by the clef to indicate that the descant sounds an octave higher than the written pitch. Played on a tenor, the part sounds as it is written.

The Note A¹ (T/D E¹)

First re-read pages 5-6 which describe the thumb position. Finger bottom A (E) o 123 45--, and play it. Keeping on playing it, slightly bend the thumb-joint of the left hand, so that the thumb-nail slips gently over the edge of its hole and rests just inside the hole, letting in a chink of air. The A (E) will jump up an octave to A¹ (E¹).

Do this in the reverse direction, letting the thumb-nail just graze the edge of its hole as the thumb slides back to the cover position. Breath-pressure should be constant: do not drop it or increase it as you change from one octave to another. Above all, do not pinch the thumb-nail into its hole. It should lie there so gently that a slight tap would knock it away.

Still fingering A¹ (E¹), and playing the note, remove the thumb-nail altogether so that it is half an inch or less below the thumb-hole. You will still be playing A¹ (E¹) but of a coarser quality because a background windy note intrudes upon the pure A¹ (E¹). Moving the thumb slowly and carefully, put it into and away from its hole, playing A¹ (E¹) continually. Practise this movement more quickly, until you can place the thumb-nail accurately every time. To move from the open to the thumbed position with accuracy and rapidity is one of the hardest but most important achievements required in recorder technique.

Finally, try the effect of gently moving the thumb-nail in its hole to increase and decrease the aperture, playing a continuous A¹ (E¹). Listen carefully to the changing quality of the note. Find where it is purest; this will probably be with the crescent-shaped area of the aperture being about an eighth of the total area of the thumb-hole.

But note that an A¹ (E¹) plays, whatever the aperture. This is not the case with higher notes, where the aperture becomes more critical. This property of A¹ (E¹) gives the recorder player time to adjust apertures in readiness for higher notes, or to take the thumb off not quite synchronized with the finger movements when playing A¹ to G¹ or F♯¹ (E¹ to D¹ or C♯¹).

In creating this small hole, the thumb is acting as a 'speaker' to induce the upper octave without the need to obtain it by over-blowing the lower octave. It enables the recorder to play softly in the upper octave. Without going too much out of tune, blow a loud A (E) in the lower octave, and a soft A¹ (E¹) an octave higher.

To sense the movements of the thumb play the following note-pattern first slowly and gradually more quickly:

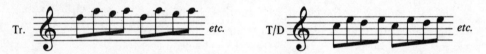

8 Thumb-hole closed. Note how little movement there is between the two thumb positions shown above and opposite. The movement should be rapid but very delicate. For thumb off position, see photograph 7 on p.22.

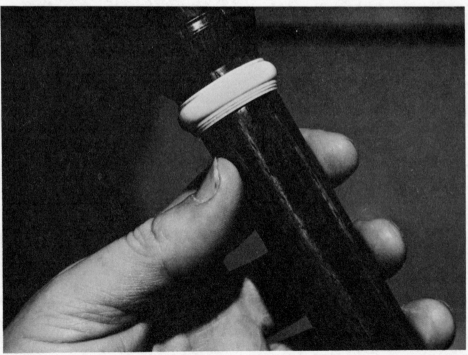

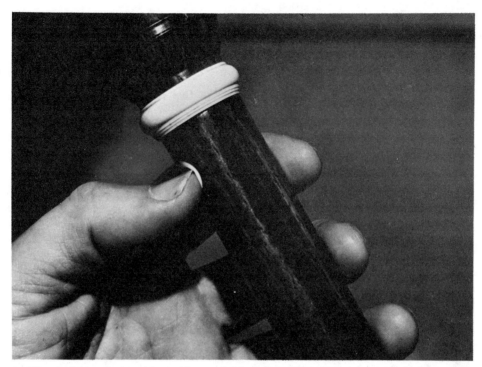

9 Thumbed (octaving) position, with one-eighth aperture (the widest aperture normally needed). Note how little movement there is between the two thumb positions shown above and opposite. The movement should be rapid but very delicate. For thumb off position, see photograph 7 on p.22.

Ex. 16 Tr. *Masque Dance* – The second of Sir John Paggingtons

Notes

1. Play first slowly with four quarter notes to the bar, ensuring that the pattern in bar 2 fits correctly into one beat. Then play rather faster with two half-note beats to the bar, leaning gently on each second beat.

2. This is No. 18 of *Twenty-one Masque Dances* for solo (treble – except No. 11 – or tenor/descant) and keyboard, published by London Pro Musica Edition, with an informative introduction.

Ex. 17 T/D Thomas Britton *Duets* No. 4 – slow (for two descants, two tenors, or descant and tenor)

Notes

1. The upper line contains the Eˡs: the second line is only for accompaniment. But to play both lines together is a good exercise both in ensemble (especially the third beat of bar 2 and the first beat of bar 7 which should sound ♪♫ when combined) and in intonation – the G♯s (see p.27) and the unison A in bar 4 in particular.

2. In bars 2 and 3 (upper line) play first without slurs from and to the Eˡs. When the thumb and finger movements are really quick, slur. The upward slur from Dˡ to Eˡ is very difficult as it creates an 'in-between note' or 'click' associated with crossing the register break (i.e. from lower to upper octave). In more advanced technique you will learn various ways of avoiding this click (see *RT* pp.62-3, 76, 85-6), but thumbing and fingering dexterity are of paramount importance. Recorders vary in the obtrusiveness of the click in slurring Dˡ to Eˡ.

3. Thomas Britton (1651-1714) was a coal-merchant who started a musical club in a room above his warehouse in Clerkenwell attended by the chief musicians of the day, such as Handel and Pepusch (of *Beggar's Opera* fame). His duets from a manuscript in the British Library are arranged by Edgar Hunt in Schott Ed. 10027. They would probably have been accompanied at the keyboard, so moderating the parallel fourths and fifths in bars 3 and 7 (which are contrary to the 'rules' of harmony and sound slightly strange).

The end of the Allemanda movement of a Corelli violin sonata arranged for descant (or tenor) recorder and keyboard by F. Koschinsky (Peters D 1283) might have been composed to cultivate facility in approaching Aˡ (Eˡ) from the lower register. Play slowly at first, especially bar 3.

Ex. 18 A. Corelli *Sonata in A minor* – extract from second movement

Transposed for Treble

repeat

repeat

The Note C¹ (T/D G¹)

Play lower octave C o 123 ----. Now move the thumb to the same position as for A¹ (E¹) (see page 32) and with moderate tonguing play C¹ (G¹) ø 123 ----. Try it with different tonguings, breath-pressures and thumbing apertures until you have the sweetest possible note, listening carefully all the time to avoid coarse background tones. You will discover that (on most recorders, at least) C¹ (G¹) will not play with the thumb off its hole. It usually needs a ⅛th aperture; this varies from one recorder to another. Play your long notes again and check the intonation of C¹ against C, A¹ and F¹ (T/D G¹ against G, E¹ and C¹). You may have to make small changes in breath-pressure to achieve notes of a perfect chord.

The following excerpts will introduce C¹ (G¹) in relation to A¹ (E¹), but you will shortly exercise C¹ (G¹) in relation to B¹ (F♯¹) and B♭¹ (F♮¹) as it is more valuable to work on the lower notes of the second octave as a group.

Keep the thumb relaxed.

Ex. 19 Tr. William Williams. Opening of *Sonata in Imitation of Birds* for two treble recorders and continuo (1703) ed. Thurston Dart (OUP)

Notes

1. Although the time-signature is C, it is at first easier to count eight eighth notes to the bar, with three beats on the first note.
2. Emphasize the thirty-second notes – 'Dee-er'.
3. 'Continuo' in 18th-century music usually means keyboard (harpsichord) and cello or bass viol (viola da gamba).

Ex. 20 T/D Anon. *Greensleeves to a Ground* for descant recorder and keyboard ed. Dolmetsch (Schott)

Notes

1. Speed is gently moving: note how the accentuation – · · gives forward movement.
2. The recorder is accompanying the keyboard which has the theme for the first time in these variations (this is No. 4). Play the theme and then try to hear it as you play the top line.
3. Even though marked *f*, do not play the G¹s in bar 5 forcefully – they are all part of the embroidery to the theme.
4. For playing *p* and *f*, see Ex. 26 note 4.

The Notes B¹ and B♭¹ (T/D F♯¹ and F¹)

B¹ (T/D F♯¹)   ø 123 –5——
B♭¹ (T/D F¹)   ø 123 4–6–

Follow the same procedure as for C¹ (G¹) in order to discover optimum tonguing, breath-pressure and thumbing. Thumbing aperture is normally about ⅛th. B¹ (F♯¹) needs thumbing to strike, but a coarse B♭¹ (F¹) can be played on most instruments with no thumbing. Thumbing aperture is not critical for either note (i.e. a slightly inaccurate thumb placing so that the aperture is less or greater than optimum will not prevent the note from striking).

Note that cross-fingering in the upper octave normally requires *one finger* below the open hole, while in the lower octave *two* holes are covered below the open one. Test, by concentrating on long notes, octave intonation accuracy between B and B¹ (F♯ and F♯¹) and between B♭ and B♭¹ (F and F¹). Play octaves fairly quickly to get used to the feel of removing 6 for the B (F♯) octaves and 7 for the B♭ (F) octaves. Test, by long notes, intonation of the arpeggio F – B♭ – D – F¹ – B♭¹ (T/D C – F – A – C¹ – F¹) and of the arpeggio G – B–D–G¹ – B¹ (D – F♯ – A – D¹ – F♯¹).

If you can play C to B♭ (G – F) accurately in the lower octave (three-finger movement) you should have no difficulty with the same transition in the upper octave (two-finger movement), but any uncertainty in finding or covering the holes simultaneously which may be exposed by the following exercises should be cured by the 'discover, press, relax, hammer' method.

The A¹ to B♭¹ (E¹ to F¹) movement is common, and is a little awkward in that 6 and 5 must move simultaneously in opposite directions, and 6 tends to move more sluggishly than 5. A bad movement in a slur will produce an ugly 'in-between note'. If you encounter this difficulty, imagine that 5 and 6 are 'walking': or that you are playing a neat slow trill with them on a keyboard instrument. Where fingers move in opposite directions you may find it helps to concentrate more on the fingers coming up than on those going down.

Next try all the movements up and down from F¹ to each of A¹, B♭¹, B♮¹ and C¹ (T/D C¹ to each of E¹, F¹, F♯¹ and G¹), keeping the thumb movement crisp but gentle; and then from G¹ to A¹, B♭¹, B♮¹ and C¹ (T/D from D¹ to E¹, F¹, F♯¹ and G¹) keeping the thumb-nail traverse short but accurate – do not push the thumb-nail into the hole, just let it alight there on each move, like a bird upon a twig.

All this should be consolidated by exercises. These notes occur frequently as they are in a tonal area where recorders are effective with other instruments.

Treble Exercises
Ex. 21 Tr. George Bingham *Suite in E minor* for treble and keyboard (c. 1704)
ed. Tilmouth (Schott 'Series' 55) – first movement (Air)

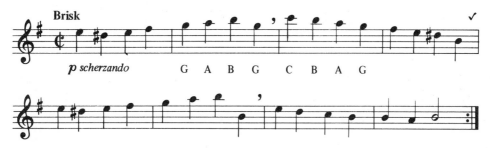

Notes
1. The notes are marked under bars 2 and 3 as notes above G use 'ledger lines', which are sometimes confusing to the eye.

38

2. Play F#¹ throughout.
3. Reminder – D# 0 1–3 4–––
4. This 'Air' is in fact a Gavotte with its square two in a bar bounce.

Ex. 22 Tr. Godfrey Finger *Suite No. 2 in G* for three trebles ed. Bergmann (Schott Lib. 49) – start of second movement

Play with a firm, pushing rhythm, emphasizing the dotted notes.

Ex. 23 Tr. Benedetto Marcello *Sonata in B flat* ed. Pearson (OUP) – start of first movement

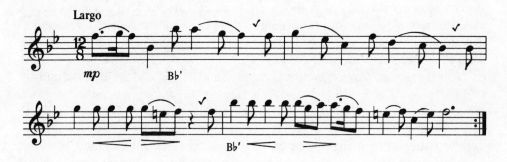

Notes
1. Siciliana – four slow but lilting beats in a bar, each divided in three.
2. Nimble fingering is needed for the slurs. Do not overlook the E♭ in bar 2.
3. Take a full breath at the quarter note rest for the long phrase that follows.

Ex. 24 Tr. Heinrich Isaac *Alla Bataglia* (four-part consort) (London Pro Musica Ed.) – Superius part, last ten bars

Notes

1. Play this quite fast – older music is frequently in half-note beats and therefore looks slower than it is.
2. Note the device of playing the same theme at double the speed. One must always look for things of this kind in consort music.
3. In bar 4 the F¹ is sharp – the sharp has been added by the editor (see Ex. 26 note 3). Stress the quarter note G¹ at the beginning of this bar (see note on Ex. 11).
4. Note the tie near the end across the bar-line – it creates a momentary rhythmic hiccup. The last note marked ⌒ (=prolong) is held on beyond its two beats.
5. Isaac (1450-1517) was a Flemish composer; battle pieces were popular at the time.

Further treble pieces for practice up to C¹
    G. F. Handel *Pieces for treble recorder* (Schott 2563A) Nos. 7, 8, and 13
    Masque Dances of the early 17th. c. (Pro Musica) Nos. 5, 8, and 15
    B. Marcello *Sonata in B flat* (OUP) – Largo, Gavotta and Minuetto

Tenor/Descant Exercises

Ex. 25 T/D Thomas Britton *Duets* No. 1 – Borée

Notes

1. For notes on the Bourrée see Ex. 13. Play this in $\frac{4}{4}$ time until you are sure of the notes, when it can go just fast enough to establish a two half-note beat. Play very lightly and jerkily.
2. The upper line exercises C♯¹, D¹, E¹, F♯¹, and G¹. The lower line should be played as well. Get to know both lines well enough to be able mentally to hear one while you play the other, keeping half an eye on the stave you are not playing. Unlike the other Britton piece (Ex. 17) this has no strange harmonies, for it is mostly in parallel thirds (two notes apart), which sound nice.
3. Play on two tenors, two descants, descant and tenor, or descant and treble.

Ex. 26 T/D Henry VIII 'Pastime with Good Company' ed. Dolmetsch from *Six pieces for three recorders* (D. Tr. T.) (Universal)

Notes

1. The half-note beat is fast (though as always play slowly until you are sure of the notes and fingerings) – see Ex. 24 note 1.

2. At full speed, the C¹ – B♭ slur in the penultimate bar is very difficult to accomplish with normal fingerings. Just do your best for the time being. More advanced technique will show you how to get round such difficulties (*RT* p.81).

3. If the renaissance convention of 'musica ficta' applies (see the editorial sharp in Ex. 24), the leading notes in the minor key or mode are sharpened at cadences even if not shown by the composer, and the ending might be as shown in square brackets. This makes a slightly easier eighth-note slur. (See 'musica ficta' in *The Oxford Companion to Music*).

4. When you repeat *p*, reduce your breath-pressure only fractionally, otherwise there will be a noticeable flattening in pitch. Try to produce the effect of repeating softly by shortening each note *slightly*, and by reducing the level of attack (tonguing). Ask a truthful friend if he hears your change of dynamic, and if he thinks you have gone flat; or listen to yourself on a tape-recorder. The recorder's dynamic range is much more restricted than that of most other instruments, so do not attempt too marked a difference between *f* and *p*, for nothing is nastier than a flat echo. More advanced techniques will increase dynamic range a little (see *RT* Chapters VII and X).

Ex. 27 T/D Anthony Holborne *The Honie Suckle* ed. Parkinson (Schott Archive 17)

Notes

1. See Ex. 15 for Holborne. Play in a lively and extrovert manner, but not loud, i.e. at a generally low breath-pressure, or you would not hear what is going on in the

four lower parts. The piece goes quite quickly. Repeat softly, bearing in mind Ex. 26 note 4.

2. Although breath-marks are given, additional phrasing (') is needed. Put this in to achieve balanced phrases. In consort music phrase-marks do not usually occur at the bar-line.
3. Note the 'hiccups' or syncopations at the end. Play them without emphasis, as if the two penultimate bar-lines had been moved one quarter note to the right.
4. The F¹ three bars from the end after the tied G¹ is natural, not sharp.

Ex. 28 T/D Thomas Leetherland 'Pavan' from *Jacobean Consort Music* Book 5 (Stainer and Bell) – second strain

Notes
1. This is the top part of a six-part consort.
2. A Pavan is a processional dance in three sections or 'strains', and even when it is transmuted into intense chamber music, as here, it should go with a stately slow swing. But do not count too firmly, for much of the phrasing is across bar-lines.
3. Watch carefully which F¹s are natural and which are sharp.

Further tenor/descant pieces for practice up to G¹
Bergmann *Descant Recorder Lessons* (Faber) Nos. 64-85, and 88
Fifty Old Airs and Dances from Scotland and Ireland (Schott) Nos. 14, 15 and 20
Henry VIII *Six Pieces* (Universal) – Fantasie I, and 'Pastime with Good Company' (complete)
Anthony Holborne *Suite for five recorders* (Schott Archive 17) – Galliard, and The Night Watch

The Note A♭¹ or G♯¹ (T/D E♭¹ or D♯¹)

This note lies between registers, and can therefore be something of a problem. Normal fingering is usually given as – –23 456–. Play whole notes with varying breath-pressures and light tonguing to see how the note sounds. Check it for intonation against F¹ (C¹) and F♯¹ (C♯¹). The interval between F♯¹ and A♭¹ or G♯¹ (T/D between C♯¹ and E♭¹ or D♯¹) should be one tone: but F♯¹ (C♯¹) often tends to be a little flat so be cautious before blaming the G♯¹ (D♯¹).

The note may sound coarse, with discordant breathy undertones too prominent in the background. If so, try it with the first finger of the left hand down – 123 456–.

This is fractionally flatter: the tone may be inferior, but it could be an improvement. So much depends on each individual recorder.

If neither of these A♭'s (E♭'s) is adequate, try the thumbed version ø 123 45⁶–, using the half-hole on 6. This is sweeter, but could be fractionally sharp.

For the time being settle on one of these A♭'s (E♭'s) (it will usually be – –23 456–) as your normal fingering. When you reach a more advanced stage you will begin to use the alternative fingerings to improve intonation, achieve a wider range of dynamics, or to shape a phrase more musically (see *RT* pp.74-8).

Ex. 29 Tr. Robin Milford *Christmas Pastoral* for treble recorder and piano (1957) (OUP) – extract

Notes

1. This piece uses both G♯' and A♭' (Bar 4 contains a 'chromatic' passage – one descending or ascending by semitones).
2. The metronome mark is ♩.=60, i.e. 60 beats to the minute or one beat per second. When you have mastered the notes, play it at this speed. 'Lift' the final quarter note of a ♩. ♪♩ phrase by shortening it slightly.
3. In the slur A' to A♭' the thumb can be moved fractionally before the fingers if the non-thumbed A♭' is used.
4. Take account of the dynamics (crescendo in bar 3, gradual diminuendo in bar 5) but not to the extent of going out of tune – listen carefully.
   > = slight stress – don't overdo it.
5. If you can play this extract, you can easily play the whole piece. Try it with a friendly pianist.

Ex. 30 T/D Henry Purcell *In Nomine à 6*, arr. Bergmann (Faber) – extract

Notes

1. A steady Andante speed. Smooth and soft.
2. Pencil accidentals above the F's and Es if you have difficulty in remembering that the accidental controls its note to the end of the bar, after which the key signature overrides it. Strictly the ♭ before the E in bar 3 is unnecessary – it is only there as a reminder.

3. One breath will be needed in the middle of this extract. Work out where it comes and pencil it in.
4. If you can play this extract, you can play the whole piece – but will need to join a consort group to gain that rich reward.

Lower Octave A♭ or G♯, (T/D E♭ or D♯), and F♯ (T/D C♯)

We have met the thumbed upper A♭¹ (E♭¹) with the half-hole ⌀. This is in fact simply an octaved lower octave A♭ (E♭). There are two ways of covering half-holes. One is to bend the finger up (i.e. with the middle joint higher than the plateau of the other fingers) and cover the hole more with the tip of the finger than the pad – but remember that 6 is normally well across the body of the instrument so one only in fact moves nearer the tip of 6. The other is to swivel the right wrist slightly, giving a fuller view to the player of the back of the right hand: the finger need not then be bent and the hole is still covered with the pad of the finger. Both methods should be learnt, although one of them is likely to feel more natural than the other. The swivel position is especially valuable where there are many A♭s (E♭s) in the music being played, for example if it is in C minor or E flat major. The swivel needs to be further round for A♭ than for F♯. Counting normal full-cover this gives three wrist positions. Experiment with both methods, in each case using the 'discover, press, relax, hammer' technique, first on A♭ (E♭), and then on F♯ (C♯).

10 Descant E♭, bending finger method. Note that the little finger remains poised above its hole (it could play an E♭-D trill).

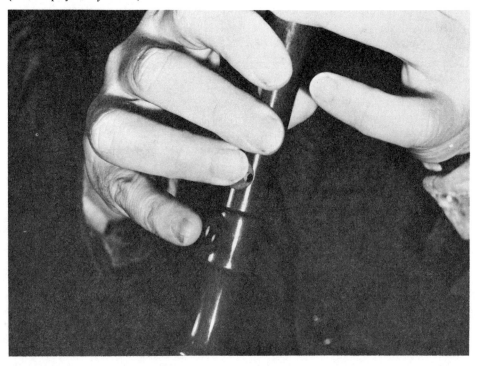

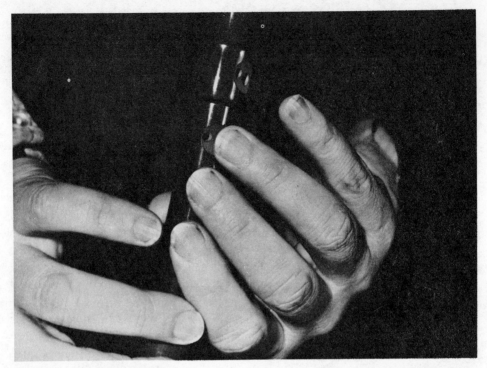

11   Descant E♭, swivel method.

Many tenor recorders have a key for bottom C. It is not then possible to play C♯. Some have both C and C♯ keys. It is a mild disadvantage to tenor players if the C♯ is missing.

Using whichever method suits your fingers best, play first slowly, and then faster and faster

Next, alternate each of these notes with C♯ (G♯), then with F♯¹ (C♯¹), as shown.

In non-advanced music you will rarely find the two half-holed notes in juxtaposition, so exercises are given for them separately, first for G♯ and A♭, then for F♯ (T/D D♯ and E♭, then C♯).

Ex. 31 Tr. John Dowland *Pavan: Lachrimae Antiquae Novae* for recorder quintet, ed. Hunt (Schott Arch. 20) – second treble part, start of third strain

Notes

1. Finger 6 covering both half-holes is needed for the B in bar one, but it comes up for the A when the hand can swivel in readiness for the G♯, and swivel back on the last A for the B at the beginning of the second bar. If the bending method is used, while the A is played 6 can move into the bent position ready to drop on its hole, and then walk back to the full cover position at the end of the bar. The movement should feel good, almost as though it were itself interpreting the music.

2. Greater technical difficulties than this do not often present themselves in Dowland's wonderful *Lachrimae or seaven Teares figured in seaven passionate Pavans* (1605). To play this music well, rhythmic sensitivity is needed, and the ability to hear a complex texture of parts while sustaining one's own line.

Ex. 32 J. S. Bach *Sonata for Solo Flute*, arr. Dolmetsch (Universal) – beginning of Bourrée Anglaise

Notes

1. Play this slowly to practise the G to A♭ slur in the last two bars. Rapid swivelling will drag 6 from full to half cover.

2. The Sonata as a whole is so musically rewarding and technically difficult as to last a recorder player a lifetime of study.

Ex. 33 T/D 13th. c. Motet (dance-song) for three recorders from *Gothic Music* (Moeck/Universal Zfs 300) – top part from beginning

Notes

1. See penultimate bar. As 6 is needed for F♯ there is very little time to position for D♯. This will test whether you prefer the bending finger or the swivelling method.

2. The triplet must be neat and exactly within one quarter note at a fast speed. Try tonguing 'doodle-der'.

3. This piece is, like much medieval music, in three-part form, but is effective as a solo with percussion accompaniment.

Ex. 34 T/D Francis Baines *Variations on an old pavan for two recorders* (Schott Ed. 10463)

Notes

1. Francis Baines's variations for two descant or tenor recorders are designed to show various musical devices. This is the second section of 'Saraband in a minor key'. Play both lines.
2. The E♭ in the second line is immediately followed by D. If you use the swivel method, push 6 across with the wrist movement. For the bending finger method, straighten the finger joint slightly but sharply to resume full coverage.
3. Study both parts to find where best to take breath, and pencil phrase-marks in.
4. If another player is not available, and you have a tape-recorder, try playing 'with yourself'. Count aloud '1 2 3' before starting, and record the lower part. On replay you then know when to start the upper part.

Ex. 35 Tr. Orlando Gibbons *Three Fantasias for two treble recorders* ed. Ritchie (Faber) – Fantasie III (excerpt)

Notes

1. Play both parts, using an exact but unplodding four quarter-note beat. After practice, relax into a more flexible half-note beat. Bar-lines were post-Renaissance, but modern editors often add them.

2. Phrase both parts in pencil, so that the phrasing matches. Look for four-note phrases, and identical rhythmic patterns. Phrasing between repeated notes (even eighth notes) is common.

3. If another player is not available, use a tape-recorder. Record the lower part. Try and follow both lines at once.

4. Music is always printed so that notes played together align vertically. This helps in reading music of this kind.

5. The approach to the F♯ in each case allows the right hand to be in the slight swivel position so that the little finger can cover its half-hole in the same straight position as it normally covers the full hole: or for the little finger to hook itself back in the bending method.

Ex. 36 T/D John Wilbye *Fantasia à 6* arr. Wailes (Schott Arch. 43) - opening theme for descant I and tenor

Notes
1. A fine broad opening theme to a superb and technically easy piece of music.
2. Prepare the hand or little finger for the C♯ while playing the preceding E and D.

Use of half-holes for tuning

If a note is sharp, covering a half-hole beneath will flatten it. Compare your E (B) and C♯ (G♯), using the same breath-pressure. There is a likelihood that the C♯ (G♯) will be sharp – but not necessarily, for each recorder has its individual characteristics. If it is, try C♯ (G♯) o 12– 456̶. You might even need o 12– 456– to get this note in tune, i.e. covering all 6. The flattening effect of an added half-hole is greater in the upper register. A sharp C�X (G⏋) can be flattened by adding only the little finger half-hole (ø 123 – –⤳).
See Chapter V I I 'Intonation' in *Recorder Technique*.

The Note D⏋ (T/D A⏋)

To octave D⏋ (A⏋) ø 12– – – – –, a rather closer thumbing aperture is usually needed than for C⏋ (G⏋). Experiment by changing the thumbing aperture, and you will discover the extent to which thumbing is critical for this note on your instrument. With a half-open thumb-hole, D⏋ (A⏋) can rarely be coaxed to strike. On some instruments thumbing for D⏋ (A⏋) is extremely critical, i.e. the thumb must be absolutely in the optimum position for the note to play.

You will also notice that D⏋ (A⏋), unlike C⏋ (G⏋), gets slightly sharper with widening the aperture. This can be used to tune the note, particularly against lower octave D (A). If thumbing is critical, the thumb move for intonation purposes must be done a split second after the note strikes.

Your experimentation will show that tonguing is also critical for D¹ (A¹). Use the gentlest tonguing that will securely and clearly start the note. Treble players will note that D¹ rests above the second ledger line above the stave. For tenor and descant players, A¹ is the first note above the stave to use a ledger line.

The Note C♯¹ (T/D G♯¹)

Like B¹ (F♯¹) and B♭¹ (F¹), C♯¹ (G♯¹) is made by a one-below fork fingering, thus ø 12– 4---.

Once again experiment to discover the qualities and intonation of C♯¹ (G♯¹) on your own recorder. You will probably find:

(a) that the thumbing aperture is the same as for D¹ (A¹);

(b) that tonguing is extremely critical – too much tonguing causes a higher note to want to strike, too little will induce a lower octave note;

(c) that there is some sharpening effect by widening thumbing aperture, but less than for D¹ (A¹).

Always remember that tonguing and breath-pressure do not need to relate. A note such as bottom F (C) requiring light tonguing can, the split second after it strikes, be given a high breath-pressure to make it louder (and sharper). And the obverse of this, strong tonguing followed by low breath-pressure, is, together with relaxed thumbing, the secret of playing high notes softly.

Exercises for D¹ and C♯¹ (T/D A¹ and G♯¹) now follow.

Ex. 37 Tr. Anthony Holborne *Heigh-ho Holiday* (five-part consort) (Schott Arch. 17) – first section, treble 1 part

Notes

1. No speed indication is given but this excerpt is followed by a fast $\frac{6}{8}$ section. A steady three (Andante) would contrast nicely. Play it gently, as the tune is in the descant part.
2. Play with a descant player, or failing that play the tune yourself (sounding an octave lower), and imagine the descant part while you play your own line.
3. Study both parts to discover where to phrase.
4. Bar 3 is rhythmically complex. Count six eighth notes '123456' for this bar only.

Ex. 38 Tr. G. F. Handel *Sonata in G minor* for treble and continuo ed. Hunt (Schott) – end of last movement

Not too fast, as the continuo bass is all in eighth notes.

Ex. 39 Thomas Ravenscroft *Fantasia No. 4* (five-part) ed. Steinitz (Schott Bib. 25) – descant 1 and treble parts from bar 3

Notes

1. Note the accidentals carrying through the bar.
2. Follow 'in your mind's ear' the other part – at least during the rests.

Ex. 40 J. H. Schmelzer *Sonata for 7 recorders* ed. Meyer (Schott Ed. 10105) – descant 1 part, start of last section

Loud–medium tonguing and high breath-pressure. 'The Schmelzer' is a particular favourite with recorder groups, though it is more difficult to bring off than it looks.

The Note E♭¹ (T/D B♭¹)

Recorder acoustics now get complicated as there is an 'upward break' beyond D¹ (A¹) induced by cross-fingering. Treble E♭¹ (with the third ledger-line above the stave through it) or tenor/descant B♭¹ (lying on the first ledger-line above the stave) are fingered ø 12– 456–. Thumbing aperture is usually a little less critical than for D¹ (A¹) for starting the note, but has considerable effect on intonation. Tonguing is also less critical, but aim at a medium tonguing as for D¹ (A¹). With medium breath-pressure, experiment by moving the thumb around to find the sweetest note that is in tune with bottom E♭, G¹ and B♭¹ (T/D B♭, D¹ and F¹). On many recorders E♭¹ (B♭¹) has a limpid quality. It is one of the most comfortable high notes to play, and being cross-fingered is easily adjustable for intonation (*RT* p.94).

Ex. 41 Tr. H. Purcell *In Nomine à 6* arr. Bergmann (Faber) – treble 1 part, from first entry

Play this softly, so that it would not over-dominate the other parts, especially at bar 4 where the bass has an important entry.

Ex. 42 T/D G. F. Handel *Sonata in Bb* ed. Dart/Bergmann (Schott Ser. 20) – second half of first movement

Notes
1. This Sonata from the Fitzwilliam Museum, Cambridge, is for oboe and continuo. It was perfectly allowable in Handel's time to use another instrument for a sonata where it was suited to the style of the music.
2. The theme of the movement is restated four bars from the end. The last Bb¹ is the climax of the movement. Play it with confidence and elegance.
3. Although marked $\frac{4}{4}$, the bass movement is in eighth notes, and the soloist can count eight freely flowing eighth notes to the bar.

The Note E¹ (T/D B¹)

E¹ (T/D B¹), normally fingered ø 12– 45– –, usually strikes best with a thumbing aperture as for D¹ (A¹) or fractionally wider, and a medium to strong tonguing. At its optimum thumbing, the note may be flat, so a split-second widening of the aperture to raise the pitch may be needed.

Ex. 43 Tr. Orlando Gibbons' Fantasia II from *Two four-part Fantasias* ed. Gardner (Schott Bib. 41) – treble part, bars 44-50

Notes

1. Quite fast. The editor suggests two beats in the bar, ♩ =76. You will need sureness of rhythm, particularly at the end of the phrase, to manage this.
2. Notes of the altitude of E¹ are not often encountered in consort music.

Ex. 44 T/D 'Sir Francis Bacon's Masque 1' No. 5 from *Twenty-one Masque Dances of the 17th c.* (Pro Musica) – second section

Notes

1. Mark the phrasing. Establish the speed by considering what suits the music best. Play springily.
2. See Ex. 16. All the pieces in this book go well on tenor or descant recorders.

Top F¹¹ (T/D C¹¹) Top G¹¹ (T/D D¹¹)

F¹¹ (C¹¹) ø 1-- 45--
   Thumbing is very critical – but relax!
   Medium to strong tonguing.
   Experiment. This note often needs coaxing.

G¹¹ (D¹¹) Usually ø 1-3 4-6-, but experiment, e.g. adding 7.
   Thumbing usually as for E¹ (B¹).
   Strong tonguing. Usually strikes well.
   For more on high notes, including the controversial F♯¹¹ (C♯¹¹), see *RT*, Chapter IX.

Tenor/descant players who have reached the point of venturing to top B's and C''s should study the whole of *Greensleeves to a Ground* (see Ex. 20). Top D''s are very rare, and on a descant can be unpleasantly shrill.

Treble players could have their first experience of high notes by playing Louis Quentin's attractive Aria for treble and piano (Schott Ser. 25). High treble notes are common in Telemann and Bach.

Alternative E (T/D B)

Play the following with normal fingering F¹ (C¹) o −2− −−−− and E (B) o 1−− −−−−

Now play it with E (B) o −23 −−−−. This involves a one-finger movement (with 3), instead of a two-finger movement in contrary motion. Test the two Es (Bs) to compare intonation and tone-quality. Even if the difference is significant − and on many recorders it is not − the facility of the alternative fingering will justify its use, at least in a fast passage. It will certainly do so when the above passage is played fast enough to become a trill (beginning, as here, on the upper note). Alternative fingerings are sometimes referred to as 'trill fingerings'. For a full treatment of alternative fingerings see *RT*, Chapter VIII.

Ex. 45 Tr. J. S. Bach Tenor aria 'Sanfte soll' from the *Easter Oratorio* – treble 1 part from the opening for two treble recorders

Notes
1. Eight eighth notes in the bar, flowingly.
2. The E's marked x are easier to slur to with E o −23 −−−−. You may also find the alternative E more comfortable at (x).

Ex. 46 T/D Samuel Scheidt *Canzona* 'Bergamasca' (five-part) ed. Garff (Bärenreiter HM 96) – top part, bars 68-69

Notes
1. The time-signature suggests a very lively speed, but count four to start with.

2. Slurring would have made the use of the alternative B o –23 –––– an absolute necessity, but even unslurred at this speed it is easier to use the alternative B where marked x. Use normal fingering for the last two Bs.
3. If the piece had been slower, use of the alternative B would have depended on its intonation and tone-quality.

On fingering

While the hammering method familiarizes you with the position of the holes on the recorder and strengthens independent finger muscles, your ultimate objective should be to finger and thumb lightly. Fingers and thumb should move in their short traverse like well-oiled pistons, but with the lightness of a butterfly's wings. And in a fast piece such as the last exercise, they should almost dance to the music. As you become more experienced, you will find ways of economizing in movement without loss of accuracy or control. For example, you may adopt a finger traverse of less than an inch, or you may experiment in thumbing octaves without using the thumb-nail - which prevents thumb-hole wear.

Advancing Further

If you have worked through this book, you will have learnt the rudiments of music (if you could not read music before), you will know the normal fingerings for all the notes of the recorder (and one alternative), and you will be acquainted with the individual characteristics and qualities of your own recorder. You will have learned habits of posture, fingering, thumbing, tonguing, and breath-control that can form the basis of a good advanced technique. And in the process you will have been introduced to musicianship, which involves accurate relaxed reading, listening to other parts, the shaping of phrases, knowing where to take breath, and studying and interpreting recorder music of different styles and periods.

Having come this far, advancing further is for the time being more a question of experiencing music than of technique, though if you move outside the broad field of consort music you will before long encounter problems of interpretation - and especially ornamentation - for which you will need the kind of technical advice given in *Recorder Technique* and elsewhere. At present, however, your main concern is to familiarize yourself with reading and playing recorder music.

Except in pieces that are often technically difficult (see Ex. 32), the recorder cannot make music on its own. You will therefore need to join a group of other players; what music you play, and how your interests develop, will then largely depend on them.

Playing in a recorder group

If you can make a reasonable attempt at most of the exercises and practice material in this book, you are ready to join the U.K. Society of Recorder Players, the American Recorder Society, or the equivalent in your country, and should not hesitate to do so. The A.R.S. has some 65 chapters spread across the United States. There are S.R.P. branches in most parts of the U.K., meeting at least monthly, sometimes weekly. Membership ranges from experienced players (who will take their turn in conducting) to relative newcomers. Branches vary in size, but a meeting of 20-40 players is typical. This is large enough to accommodate newcomers – you will not be expected to hold a part on your own, or even to play every note. For part of a meeting, larger societies may break into groups designed to help beginners.

A local library information centre or music shop will usually put you in touch with the secretary of the local S.R.P. branch, or you can contact the Local Education Authority Music Adviser who may also know of groups outside the S.R.P. A list of S.R.P. branch secretaries is in each issue of *Recorder and Music* (48 Great Marlborough Street, London WIV 2BN), and of chapter representatives of A.R.S. in its quarterly *The American Recorder* (141 West 20th Street, New York, NY 10011). A function of the A.R.S. and the S.R.P. is to put players in touch with each other, so that those of roughly equivalent competence can meet privately. As a newcomer, try to join with a group comprising at least one player with enough experience to recognize where things go wrong, and how to put them right. You will then learn from him, and in turn pass on your understanding to other new players.

What you play at S.R.P. and other meetings will depend on the group's repertoire. You are likely to encounter the music represented by Exercises 15, 24, 26, 27-8, 30-31, 33, 35-7, 39-41, 43, and 46, together with antiphonal (two or more 'choirs' answering each other) music by Gabrieli and his contemporaries, and probably arrangements from Purcell, Handel, and Bach, with an occasional 20th-century piece. It is extremely important that you practise the music between meetings.

At S.R.P. meetings you will occasionally have the chance of playing with keyboard or other instruments.

In ensemble playing especially, good intonation is imperative. Small adjustments can be made by a slight increase or decrease of breath-pressure. Single notes can be corrected by little-finger shading or other devices (see *RT*, Chapter VII). The pitch of the recorder can be flattened slightly by 'pulling out' the middle joint (*RT* p.72), but no more than an eighth of an inch; pulling out more than this makes notes on the instrument intolerably out of tune with each other.

Playing for a long period can cause the windway of the recorder to become clogged with moisture, but this should not happen if the recorder is at body warmth before starting to play. If it does occur, 'blow out' by blowing hard, with the finger across the air-flow but not actually touching the 'window' or lip of the recorder head-piece. As soon as the opportunity arises, take the recorder apart, dry the bore out thoroughly with a recorder mop or cloth (not one that leaves bits). Some recorders are more prone to clogging than others.

In large ensemble playing you will learn to respond to the beat and the interpretations of a conductor. You have to be aware both of him, and of the other parts being played in the piece, as well as your own part. The effort is considerable, but so is the reward.

Playing with accompaniment

You may already have persuaded, as suggested, a pianist friend to accompany you in practice material, and wish to continue playing together; or playing with keyboard may be your special interest or, by force of circumstances, your only possibility of making music. The choice of music is then likely to be yours.

The exercises and practice material in this book, which will serve as a starting point, are drawn from the lists of the main publishers or agents of recorder music (in the U.K. Bärenreiter, Faber Music, Peters Edition, London Pro Musica, OUP, Schott, and Universal Edition). Write for their recorder music catalogues. Some grade pieces from easy to difficult.

A treble player's objective will probably be Handel's Opus 1 and Fitzwilliam Sonatas, some movements of which are of only moderate difficulty, though to play any baroque sonata in the style and with the ornamentation of the period requires substantial study and technique. Make progress to these via the Fughettas arranged by H. G. Weiler from Handel's keyboard works (Schott Ed. 3664). Of J. B. Loeillet's sonatas, Op. 1 No. 1 (Bärenreiter HM 43) is perhaps the most immediately rewarding.

There are also easy sonatas by Daniel Purcell (OUP and Schott) and Marcello (OUP) (see Ex. 23). Modern music is generally more difficult, but a start can be made with Robin Milford's *Three Airs* (OUP – see also Ex. 29) and Antony Hopkins's *Four Dances* (Schott Ser. 26). Do not overlook the repertoire for two treble recorders and keyboard, including several Telemann trio-sonatas; try Herbert Murrill's *Piece for my Friends* (U).

The repertoire for descant recorder and keyboard is less wide-ranging. Although descant and piano go well together, the piano overpowers the tenor recorder, which needs harpsichord (or guitar) accompaniment. Music for descant or tenor with keyboard includes Telemann's six partitas (*Kleine Kammermusik*) (Bärenreiter HM 47), the much easier sonatas of James Hook (Schott), and a fairly simple 20th-century piece, Benjamin Burrow's *Suite* (Schott Ed. 10471).

Solo playing requires a wider range of expression and of tone-colour than consort playing, and this will involve the use of different levels of vibrato (*RT* pp.56-8 and 108-9).

Duets and Trios

You may only be able to play with one or two other recorder players; or you may do this in addition to consort playing. If at all possible, try to join up with a better player than yourself; and, if you have any choice, avoid playing the top or leading part for the time being.

Publishers' catalogues offer a wide choice of duets and trios. A treble duo will eventually aspire to Telemann's sonatas (start with the one in C major from *Der*

Getreuer Musicmeister) (Schott Lib. 7). Treble trios will turn to J. Mattheson's sonatas (Schott Lib.). Descant and tenor duos will enjoy Morley's Canzonets (OUP), and there are plenty of arrangements and modern trios for D. Tr. T., including Hindemith's Trio (quite difficult).

Solo recorder

When you play on your own it should mainly be to practise pieces in preparation for ensemble playing (see *RT*, Chapter XIII). Too much playing on your own, especially at the early stages, can result in insensitive ensemble playing, and inexact rhythm. A metronome will help to cure the latter but is an unsympathetic accompanist for long periods. Playing music with a strong rhythm, such as country dances, is valuable.

A player condemned to isolation can try playing with gramophone records if both music and recording are available, preferably in concerted works without too much free ornamentation such as Bach cantatas, of which 22 have recorder parts (*RT* pp.19–20). Four Telemann duets, some Handel and Telemann solo and trio-sonatas, the eight Mattheson trios, and some renaissance dances, with a treble part missing (music provided), are recorded in the *Music Minus One* series (43 West 61st Street, New York 23; Forsyth, 126 Deansgate, Manchester 3 (U.K. distributors); or order from Henry Stave and Co., 11 Great Marlborough Street, London W1), and there is some recorder music in the M.M.O. flute list.

Solo treble players may graduate to Telemann's *Fantasias* (Schott Ed. 4734), and to *Preludes and Voluntaries* (1708) (Schott Ed. 10133) and *Fifteen Solos* (Ed. 2562A) which can please even when played slowly. Tenor and descant soloists may turn to Jacob van Eyck's *Der Fluiten Lust-Hof* (1646) for sets of variations on popular tunes of the period.

Medieval and renaissance music: playing wide-bore recorders

While early music is technically easy (discounting florid ornamentation), it is often rhythmically complex. A start should be made on simple renaissance dances (e.g. Praetorius or Susato).

Your acceptability in an early music consort will be enhanced if you possess a wide-bore recorder. Understanding its qualities, which, as always, you must discover for yourself, will lead to certain changes in technique. First, a wide-bore instrument draws more air from you, and you must feed this characteristic by expelling more breath (not necessarily at higher breath-pressure, although this depends on the voicing of the instrument). *Imagine* a wider 'oo' shape for your lips than you adopt for the baroque recorder. You will want to make the most of the rich lower notes by playing louder, so be extrovert in your attitude to a renaissance recorder.

Particularly with the lower instruments, you will have to look for many phrase points in the music at which to replenish breath.

You and your colleagues in an early music consort may want to exploit that characteristic of many renaissance recorders known as 'chiff', resulting from slowness of speaking at strong tonguing levels. According to the needs of the music, do not hesitate to attack phrases with these strong tonguings, which give a percussive edge to the music. But experiment with non-chiff (light) tonguings for more pensive music. Neat and varied tonguing is essential in rapid passages and unslurred ornamentation (for tonguings, see Chapter 5 of Ganassi's *Fontegara*, a recorder tutor of 1535 – Peters D. 1289).

To quote Ganassi: 'And just as a painter imitates natural effects by using various colours, an instrument can imitate the expression of the human voice by varying the pressure of the breath and shading the tone by means of suitable fingering . . . it is possible with some players to perceive, as it were, words to their music'.

Notes above G^1 (descant/tenor) are required in van Eyck's solos, but most parts in early music are within a range of one octave and a half. The writer's Moeck renaissance descant prefers ø 12 – 4567 for tongued A^1 and ø 123 – 567 for a safe $G\#^1$.

Each player will have to discover the qualities and fingering of his own instrument, and adopt a different attitude of mind to it than to a baroque recorder. He can then play with confidence, precision, and good intonation, even with capricious crumhorns or kortholts.

Changing from tenor/descant to treble, and vice versa

As soon as you know the notes and have had a few months' experience in reading music on your first instrument, you should purchase your second recorder – a treble (in F) if you have started on a descant or tenor (in C), or a C instrument if you have started on treble. The difficulty is not so much in fingering the new instrument but in reading music when a particular fingering produces a different note, e.g. o 123 – – – – is C on the treble but G on the tenor or descant. You will need concentration, patience, and practice to acquire this ability to change, but it is an essential accomplishment for a recorder player to be able to play both C and F instruments. The later the change is made, the more difficult it tends to be.

To become accustomed to the fingers being further apart or closer together, or to the use of a key on the tenor, go back to the beginning of this book and work through as if your were starting the instrument afresh, but at a much faster rate of progress.

The following hints may help you:

1. Imagine that the new recorder is a different instrument altogether – as different from your first recorder as (say) an oboe. Lock your first instrument away and do not touch it for several weeks. As you discover the individual characteristics of each note on the new recorder, even the need for some non-standard fingerings, its differentness will grow upon you.

2. In reading music use certain notes and their fingerings, such as C or G, as anchors and play the others in relation to them, thinking about the interval between the notes (two up or one down) and not whether the note is 'E' or 'B'.

3. Practise music of which you already know the tune, e.g. hymn tunes, but not music you associate with your old recorder (which should be locked away with it).

4. Practise music which moves stepwise, like much renaissance music. Avoid music with wide intervals and leaps.

5. Practise for a few moments before going to bed at night.

You may have to miss a meeting or two of your recorder group during this process. On your return, play only your new instrument. The first experience of switching back to the old instrument should be made in private practice. In each practice thereafter, work on both instruments. Do not be disheartened if you mis-read – even experienced players have occasional lapses. Let the different 'feel' of the instrument remind you of the reading changes.

Treble an octave up

Some continental music for recorders, including a substantial amount of consort music you may encounter at S.R.P. meetings, is written with the treble part an octave below normal British treble recorder notation, as follows:

This has the advantage of slightly fewer ledger lines, and a better visual relationship with the descant part above – the treble part is clearly lower than the descant. It does not, however, represent the actual pitch of the treble recorder.

Learning this transposition is less demanding than learning to change from an F to a C instrument. Notes 2 to 5 above should be applied. Use C, F¹, and C¹ as 'anchor points'.

Other size recorders

A treble player can quickly master the sopranino recorder in F an octave above treble, once he is accustomed to the bunching of the fingers. He will find pleasant practice in *The Bird Fancyer's Delight*, ed. Godman (Schott Ed. 10442). The art of sopranino playing is to make the high notes sweet, not shrill, and the low notes full, not thin; the careful application of vibrato (*RT* pp.56-8) is essential. The sopranino plays at treble notation, sounding an octave higher. Sopranino recorders must be warm before playing as the small windway easily becomes clogged with moisture.

A treble player is also better placed to make the change to the bass in F, although this involves reading a new clef. Notes 2 to 5 above again apply. Similarly the costly great bass in C is a fairly easy conversion for a tenor player. Playing a bass line is a considerable responsibility and a test of musicianship, for the bass, as no other player, hears every part of the music from the foundation of its harmonic structure. In many respects the bass part of a consort is the most rewarding to play.

Most bass recorders need coaxing, as the tonguing response is slow, and thumbing

positions are often very critical for the upper notes. These notes, and perhaps even some lower down, may not work best with standard fingerings. The scope for individuality in recorders is most apparent with basses. But however truculent the instrument may at first seem, patience and hard work will be well rewarded.

Interpretation

Certain points of interpretation of music have been touched upon in the notes to exercises in this book, for example that in baroque music a repeat is played differently (e.g. in dynamics or ornamentation), or that renaissance composers liked four-note phrases (e.g. Ex. 35). Many other points of interpretation and style will be learnt from the conductors of consort groups.

The most compelling way of considering the musical purpose and meaning of a piece of music, its style and phrasing, is to prepare it for performance (*RT*, Chapter XIV). This process makes one aware of inadequacies and lack of knowledge, for the object of performance is to communicate a player's understanding and enjoyment of a piece of music; and 'understanding' implies an attempt to realize the intentions of the composer in the context of the musical language of his time. This can partly be achieved by much listening to good interpretations of music of the period, not only recorder music but other instrumental and vocal music. Reading literature contemporary with the music, and looking at works of art and architecture, can deepen one's sense of the spirit of the time.

Reading about the music of a period will add to your understanding of a particular piece. There are several excellent books specifically on interpretation, such as Thurston Dart's *The Interpretation of Music* (Hutchinson, 1954) and Robert Donington's *A Performer's Guide to Baroque Music* (Faber, 1973). Membership of the Society of Recorder Players includes the quarterly *Recorder and Music*. Renaissance and medieval music requires special study and listening to performances by those attempting to recreate authentic sounds and interpretations. Advice on recordings is given in *Recorder and Music* and in the quarterly *Early Music* (OUP), both of which contain many articles of interest to recorder players.

Above all, having completed your initiation to the recorder through the pages of this book, you will want to develop musical understanding by playing well-edited recorder music from various periods. Chapter II of *Recorder Technique* and its supplement (pp.141-7) review the wealth of the recorder's repertoire. Your S.R.P. branch, or the music collection in a public library in a large town, will enable you to range more widely than your purse may allow. You will find that the discoveries to which you have been introduced through your simple recorder will afford you the profoundest of pleasures.